Moral Obligation of Fraternal Correction

BY THE

REVEREND JOSEPH A. COSTELLO S.M., S.T.L.

Nihil Obstat:

FRANCIS J. CONNELL, C.SS.R., S.T.D.

Censor Deputatus

Imprimi Potest:

EDWARD P. McGRATH, S.M.

Provincialis

Imprimatur:

✠ JOSEPH F. RUMMEL, S.T.D.

Archiepiscopus Novae Aureliae

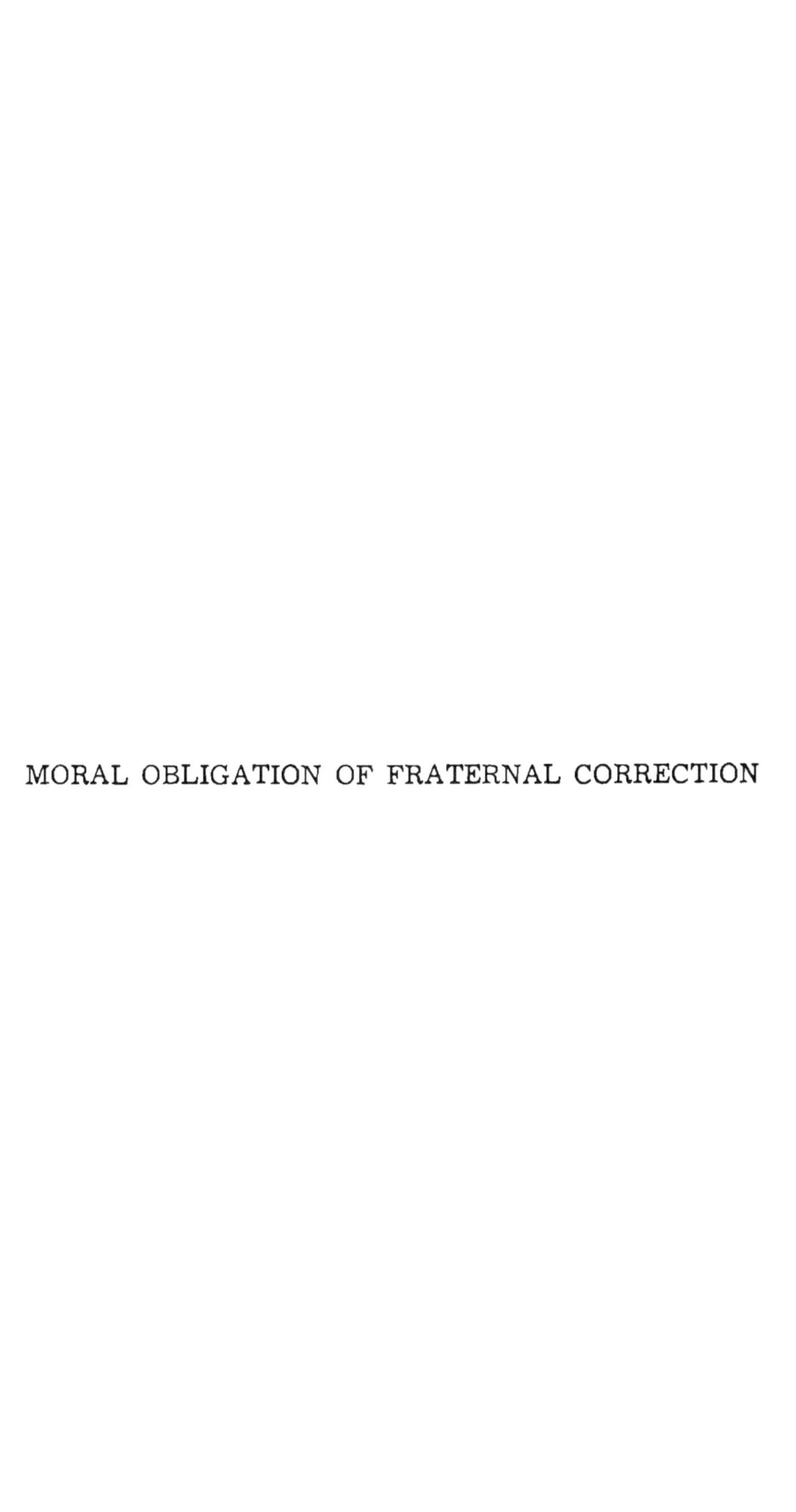

MORAL OBLIGATION OF FRATERNAL CORRECTION

TO MY MOTHER IN MEMORY

OF

MY FATHER

TABLE OF CONTENTS

INTRODUCTION

Chief among the spiritual works of mercy is fraternal correction. Many persons seem to think that the working out of one's eternal salvation is an exclusively personal task and, thus, they fail to realize that it is also a duty of brotherly love to help others attain eternal salvation. Such persons understand only one form of charity towards a neighbor—that which relieves bodily needs. They do not conceive that a neighbor can be a spiritual "pauper" and, consequently, they lack an adequate notion of their obligation to aid a neighbor in those things which pertain to his spiritual well-being. The external act of love of neighbor is often restricted to giving him aid in his temporal necessities, while the obligation to give spiritual aid, such as instruction, counsel, spiritual comfort, and fraternal correction, is either forgotten or ignored.

Since "it is therefore the duty of the faithful to know the teaching of the Church concerning fraternal correction,"[1] it is the aim of this dissertation to explain the obligation of fraternal correction; to examine the foundations of this obligation and to describe its proper fulfillment, its excellence, and its effects. The problems centering around the moral obligation of fraternal correction are many. The dissertation will attempt to answer these problems.

The plan of this work consists in presenting first the basis of the obligation—love of God and neighbor. Next follow general norms concerning the obligation to give spiritual aid to a neighbor in need. Finally, specific applications of these principles are made to the notion of fraternal correc-

[1] A. Cicognani, *The Great Commandment of the Gospel in the Early Church,* p. 305.

tion. An effort has been made to study this obligation in the light of the teaching of the Fathers and theologians. Differences of opinion on various points pertinent to this obligation are presented and evaluated, and arguments given for those views which the author regards as more probable.

The author wishes to take this occasion to express his gratitude to his religious superiors for the opportunity of pursuing graduate studies in Sacred Theology at the Catholic University. He is also deeply grateful to his major professor, Very Reverend Francis J. Connell, C.SSR., S.T.D., for his guidance and for the many helpful suggestions offered; to the Reverend Raphael Huber, O. F. M. Conv., S.T.D., S.T.M., and the Reverend Joseph C. Fenton, S.T.D., who approved the manuscript. To the members of the School of Sacred Theology and to the Reverend Gerard R. Hageman, S.M., and to all his confreres in the Society of Mary, who by their interest and aid helped in the completion of this dissertation, the writer wishes to express his gratitude and appreciation.

CHAPTER I

THE PRINCIPLE OF LOVE OF NEIGHBOR

ARTICLE I

GENERAL NOTION OF CHARITY

When our Lord was asked which was the greatest commandment, He answered:

> 'Thou shalt love the Lord thy God with thy whole heart, and with thy whole soul and with thy whole mind.' This is the greatest and first commandment. And the second is like it 'Thou shalt love thy neighbor as thyself.' On these two commandments depend the whole law and the Prophets.[1]

When dealing with this commandment of love, which in Catholic Theology is known as the commandment of charity, one enters into the realm of the supernatural. It is not out of place here to consider some fundamental notions of the supernatural order and of charity. Essentially, the Christian life is a supernatural one; this notion must be outlined.

Every real definition is the expression of our concept of the essence of a thing. In defining charity, it is necessary to differentiate between the natural and supernatural. We shall not limit ourselves to a mere nominal definition, for this is but the explanation of the *word* without regard for the nature of the thing expressed by the word. It would be insufficient to point out that the supernatural is *above* or *beyond* the natural, for this does not clearly indicate what it is essentially. However, this nominal definition has a part to play in the explanation of the concept, for it is of import to point out that *super* is not to be understood in the sense of *contra*, or against nature.[2]

[1] Matthew 22:37-40.

[2] *Cf.* H. Denzinger-C. Bannwart-J. Umberg, *Enchiridion Symbolorum Definitionum et Declarationum de Rebus Fidei et Morum,* (hereafter cited as DBU), 1635.

1

Actions spring from a motive adjusted to an end. Everyone is, to some extent, familiar with the order of nature.
Even though he be ignorant of the philosophic disciplines,
man has a general notion of the natural order. The order
of nature, as commonly understood by theologians, is "the
aggregate of all those perfections to which a created being
has a claim, each according to his specific essence."[3] Thus
man, as a rational creature, has a claim to an intellect and
will; to deny him these faculties would be a contradiction
for specifically they belong to man as man.

The mode of an action is in keeping with the form of the
agent which is the principle of the act;[4] the character of the
operation must conform to the nature of the agent placing the
act.[5] Man, in the natural order, can place acts according to
his active principles of intellect and will which bring about
an effect proportioned to the cause. Naturally, man can
know[6] and love[7] God by the use of his faculties of intellect
and will. The existence of this natural love of God, as distinct from charity, is clear from the condemned proposition
of Baius.[8] But God added to this natural knowledge and
love by giving man a supernatural destiny[9]—a *facie ad
faciem* vision of God[10]—exceeding the powers of human na-

---

[3] J. Pohle-A. Preuss, *God the Author of Nature and the
Supernatural*, p. 185.

[4] St. Thomas, *Summa Contra Gentiles*, lib. 3, c. 73: "Modus autem
agendi cujuslibet rei consequitur formam ejus, quae est principium
actionis."

[6] *Operatio sequitur esse.*

[8] *Cf.*, DBU, 1806.

[7] St. Thomas, *Summa Theologica*, I-II, q. 109, a. 3 ad 1: "Natura
enim diligit Deum super omnia, prout est principium et finis
naturalis boni."

[8] DBU, 1034: "Distinctio illa duplicis amoris, naturalis videlicet,
quo Deus amatur ut auctor naturae, et gratuiti, quo Deus amatur
ut beatificator, vana est . . . . "

[9] *Ibid.*, 1786: " Deus ex infinita bonitate sua ordinavit hominem
ad finem supernaturalem, ad participanda scilicet bona divina . . . . "

[10] 1 Corinthians 13:12.

ture.[11] New active principles were given man so that his acts would be proportioned to this End. This bestowal of new principles of activity has given man a capacity for a new kind of life—a life of intimate union with God—begun in the present life and consummated in the happiness of heaven. This life we call supernatural, for by this gift of God—*donum indebitum*—man is elevated to a specifically higher order, transcending the powers of creatures. Both the end and the means to this end are above the demand and power of creatures as far as their own nature is concerned; thus, they are supernatural.

Man, by sanctifying grace, is elevated to this new order, becoming a partaker of the divine life.[12] Grace, being the formal cause of this new life, constitutes the *principium essendi*—the principle of being—of this supernatural order, whereby the *esse* of man is elevated to the *esse supernaturale*.[13] This perfects the essence of the soul. Corresponding to this supernatural life of grace, with the infusion of grace, the Virtues of Faith, Hope and Charity are given man,[14] and these serve as the principles of action—*principia agendi*—in the supernatural order.[15] We call these virtues theological because, as St. Thomas teaches:

> their object is God, inasmuch as they direct us aright
> to God; and because they are infused by God alone,
> and because these virtues are not made known to us
> except by divine revelation contained in sacred
> scripture.[16]

[11] St. Thomas, *De Veritate*, q. 14, a. 2: "Aliud est bonum hominis naturae humanae proportionem excedens, quia ad ipsum obtinendum vires naturales non sufficiunt, nec ad cogitandum vel desiderandum; sed ex sola divina liberalitate homini repromittitur."

[12] 2 Peter 1:4.

[13] St. Thomas, *De Virtutibus In Communi*, a. 10: " Infunditur igitur divinitus homini ad peragendas actiones ordinatas in finem vitae aeternae primo quidem gratia, per quam habet anima quoddam spirituale esse . . . "

[14] Cf., DBU, 800.

[15] St. Thomas, *op. cit.*, a. 3 ad 2: " . . . esse spirituale non per virtutes est, sed per gratiam; nam gratia est principium spiritualiter essendi, virtus vero spiritualiter operandi."

[16] *Summa Theologica*, I-II, q. 62, a. 1.

Their immediate object is God in that aspect of His Divine Life which is above the perception of all created nature.[17] These virtues are essentially operative for, as St. Thomas holds, they perfect the intellect and will elevating them in such a manner that these faculties are capable of acting in a supernatural manner.[18]

Under the aspect of means to a supernatural end, charity—as a theological virtue—may be defined as:

> a divinely infused virtue by which we love God as the Supreme Good on account of Himself and ourselves and our neighbor on account of God.[19] It is love of friendship of God, by which we wish God well and desire all good for Him on account of the supreme and infinite perfection of His Divine Nature.[20]

St. Thomas treats of the notion of charity both in his commentary on the *Sentences*[21] of Peter Lombard and in his *Summa Theologica*;[22] but we shall follow the latter, since it is of a later date.[23] The teaching of the *Summa Theologica* but confirms and completes his former teaching. In both we have the complete notion of charity.

Essentially, charity is friendship of man for God.[24] Elsewhere, St. Thomas points out that charity is "some kind of friendship of man for God, by which man loves God and God loves man."[25] The basis of love of friendship, in general,

---

[17] St. Thomas, *De Virtutibus In Communi*, a. 10.

[18] *Op. cit ., loc. cit.*

[19] D. Prümmer, *Manuale Theologiae Moralis*, I, 395.

[20] St. Alphonsus, *Theologia Moralis*, (ed., Le Noir), I, 314.

[21] *In III Sent.*, dist. 27, q. 2, a. 1.

[22] II-II, q. 23, a. 1.

[23] *Cf., Basic Writings of St. Thomas Aquinas* (ed., A. Pegis), I, xlix.

[24] St. Thomas, *Summa Theologica*, II-II, q. 23, a. 1.

[25] *In III Sent.*, dist. 27 ,q. 2, a. 1: " . . . caritas, quae est quaedam amicitia hominis ad Deum, per quam homo diligit Deum, et Deus hominem . . . "

is a certain similitude of nature."[16] In charity, man has a definite relation to God based on the communication of beatitude, for God admits man to His friendship by giving him a share in the divine life.[17] The possibility of friendship between God and man was expressly denied by Aristotle,[18] but it is clear from Sacred Scripture[19] and from the teaching of the Church,[20] that love between God and man has the character of true friendship.

We have a twofold knowledge of God—natural and supernatural—and corresponding to the twofold principles of this knowledge—reason and faith—we have a twofold love of God. Love of God is natural in so far as the will goes out to Him as the Creator and Author of nature known by reason. Supernaturally, we love God by charity, in so far as He is known in His Intimate Life by the Light of Faith. Faith transcends the power of the natural intellect;[31] and charity, supernatural love of God, is beyond the power of the unaided will.[32] Thus it is clear that supernatural principles are required for this supernatural knowledge and love. The supernatural principle in the intellect is faith,

[26] St. Thomas, *Summa Theologica*, II-II, q. 23, a. 1. *Cf.*, Cicero, *Laelius* (ed., Shuckburg-Johnston), p. 14.

[27] St. Thomas, *Summa Theologica*, II-II, q. 23, a. 1: "Cum ergo sit aliqua communicatio hominis ad Deum, secundum quod nobis suam beatitudinem communicat, super hanc communicationem oportet aliquam amicitiam fundari."

[28] *Basic Works of Aristotle* (ed., R. McKeon), *Nicomachean Ethics* (Bk. 8, c. 7 nr. 1159a): " . . . when one party is removed to a great distance, as God is, the possibility of friendship ceases." p. 1066.

[29] John 15:14-15: "You are my friends . . . No longer do I call you servants, because the servant does not know what his master does. But I have called you friends, because all things that I have heard from my Father I have made known to you."

[30] DBU, 799; " . . . homo ex injusto fit justus et ex inimico amicus ut sit heres secundum spem vitae aeternae."

[31] St. Thomas, *De Veritate*, q. 14, a. 8: " . . . fides, quae virtus ponitur, faciat intellectum hominis adhaerere veritati quae in divina cognitione consistit, transcendendo proprii intellectus veritatem."

[32] St. Thomas,1, *De Caritate*, a. 2 ad 15: "Caritas non est virtus homini inquantum est homo, sed inquantum per participationem gratiae fit Deus et filius Dei."

while charity perfects the will by bringing about a supernatural union with God.[33]

Charity gives man the power to love God supernaturally and to love himself and his neighbor for the sake of God. The reason for this love, the formal motive of charity, is the Infinite Goodness of God apprehended by the light of faith.[34] The will goes out to God because of the Goodness of God considered in Itself. This Infinite Perfection of God or the Goodness of God—the reason of our love of self and neighbor as well as of God Himself—is not the Divine Goodness in as far as It benefits man,[35] but as It is considered in Itself.[36] The consideration of the Infinite Perfection of God must include, according to some theologians, the sum-total of all God's Perfections,[37] while others hold that any one of God's Perfections or Attributes considered as a Divine Goodness, is a sufficient motive for the supernatural love of God.[38]

The material object of charity is God, self, and neighbor. These are all included under the formal object since the motive for loving all is the same; but materially they are diverse.[39] The material object of charity is primarily God, but it can be extended to secondary objects in as far as these share in and reflect the Goodness of God. Thus, the act of charity by which we love God includes all those who are friends of God, those whom God loves, and with whom He shares or wishes to share His life of grace.[40] The motive for our love of neighbors is not alone their likeness to us or

[33] St. Thomas, *Summa Theologica*, I-II, q. 62. a. 3.

[34] Collegii Salmanticensis, *Cursus Theologicus, de caritate* (q. 25, disp. 2, dub. 1, n. 1). 12, 46.

[35] *Bonitas Dei relativa.*

[36] *Bonitas Dei absoluta.*

[37] Collegii Salmanticensis, *op. cit., de caritate* (q. 25, disp. 2, dub. 2, n. 14). 12, 52.

[38] C. Pesch. *Praelectiones Dogmaticae*, 8, 238.

[39] St. Thomas, *De Caritate*, a. 4 ad 1: " . . . dicendum quod proximus non diligitur nisi ratione Dei: unde ambo sunt unum objectum dilectionis, formaliter loquendo, licet materialiter duo."

[40] *Ibid.*, a. 4: " . . . proximus caritate diligitur, quia in eo est Deus, vel in eo sit Deus."

their proximity to us based on natural bonds, but because of their relation—real or potential—to God Himself.

The love of charity or of friendship is commonly opposed to the love of concupiscence or desire. St. Thomas shows that love can be directed towards two objects:

> toward the good which one wishes someone, either oneself or another,—and toward the object to which the good is wished. Toward the good which one wishes another, there is love of desire; toward the object to which one wishes good, there is love of friendship.[41]

In treating of the notion of friendship, the Angelic Doctor insists on the benevolent character of love.[42]

The second commandment is like the first; "Thou shalt love thy neighbor as thyself."[43] From this text and from the definition of charity in general,[44] we can deduce that man has another class of duties—those toward his fellow-man—of which loving him is the source and common expression. Due to a physically necessary impulse of nature, man loves himself, for his own nature can never prove unsuitable to him. It is false to assert that man has no duty to himself, on the plea that man cannot practice justice to himself. Duty is a correlative, not only of justice, but also of the other virtues. This duty of love of self is not one of justice, but of charity. The obligation of love of self is evident from the words of our Lord, for we are told to love our neighbors as ourselves, not indeed as to intensity but as to the kind of love.[45] Man loves himself for the sake of God. In like manner, for the sake of God, man loves his fellowman. The aspect under which our neighbor is to be loved is his

[41] *Summa Theologica*, I-II, q. 26, a. 4.

[42] *In X Libros Ethicorum ad Nicomachum*, lib. 8, lect. 2.

[43] Matthew 22:39.

[44] *Cf., supra*, p. 4.

[45] St. Thomas *Summa Theologica*, II-II, q. 44, a. 7: "Modus autem dilectionis tangitur cum dicitur: *sicut teipsum*, quod non est intelligendum quantum ad hoc, quod aliquis proximum sibi aequaliter diligat, sed similiter sibi . . . "

participation in the Goodness of God loved as the primary object of charity.[46] We love God because of His Absolute Goodness, by which He is Infinitely lovable for His own sake, and we love ourselves and our neighbor by reason of the fellowship—real or potential—in this same Good.[47] Thus our neighbor is loved because of his relation to God, to Whom the friendship of charity is chiefly directed.[48]

St. Thomas points out four reasons which lead us to love our fellowman with the love of charity:

> First, divine love, because "If anyone says, 'I love God,' and hates his neighbor, he is a liar." (1 Jn. 4:19.)
>
> Second, God's commandment. For Christ, at His departure, especially commended this commandment above all others. "This is my commandment that you love one another" . . . therefore this love of neighbor is a sign of the observance of divine law . . . (Jn. 15:12.)
>
> Third, the communication of nature. For it is said, Every animal loves its like." (Eccles. 13:19.) Wherefore, since all men are alike in nature, they ought to love one another. Therefore, to hate one's neighbor is contrary, not only to divine law, but also to the law of nature.
>
> Fourth, the attainment of profit. For all things of one are at the service of another by charity, for it is this which unites the Church.[49]

This love of our neighbor is based on his relation to God established in the fellowship of eternal happiness. This

[46] *Ibid.,* II-II, q. 25, a. 1: "Ratio autem diligendi proximum Deus est; hoc enim debemus in proximo diligere, ut in Deo sit."

[47] *Ibid.,* II-II, q. 26, a. 4: " . . . homo seipsum diligit ex charitate secundum rationem qua est particeps praedicti boni; proximus autem diligitur secundum rationem societatis in isto bono . . "

[48] *Ibid.,* II-II, q. 23, a. 1 ad 2: " . . . amicitia charitatis . . in ordine ad Deum, ad quem principaliter habetur amicitia charitatis."

[49] *In Duo Praecepta Caritatis Et In Decem Legis Praecepta Expositio,* opus, 3, c. 7.

love is distinguished from natural love of neighbor, for it transcends mere natural characteristics and bases itself on some good which has a direct supernatural reference to God. The principal goods which we strive to contemplate in our fellow man are: God's love for him, his adoptive sonship, and his supernatural destiny in heaven.

The supernatural character of fraternal love is abundantly evidenced by the fact man loves his neighbor for God's sake and thus his love for neighbor is a holy love; a righteous love, for he loves his neighbor only for good; a true love, for fraternal love is directed to a neighbor, not because of one's own advantage or pleasure, but because it wishes a neighbor well.[50] God is the principle of our love of neighbor;[51] and it can be shown that this love of neighbor *propter Deum* is not a virtue specifically distinct from charity towards God since the formal object of both is the same, but it is distinguished only by its material object. Truly, charity is love of God, self, and neighbor; but charity is one. It has but one formal motive—the Infinite Perfection of God. The formal motive of our love of neighbor, or the reason why we love him, is the Infinite Perfection or Goodness of God.[52]

St. Thomas points out this specific unity of charity towards God and neighbor.[53] The reason for this specific unity is clear. For

habits are not differentiated except their acts are of a different species. For every act of the one species belongs to the same habit. Now since the species of an act is derived from its object, considered under its formal aspect, it follows of necessity that it is specifically the same act that tends to an aspect of the object and tends to the object under that

[50] *Cf.,* St. Thomas, *Summa Theologica,* II-II, q. 44, a. 7.

[51] St. Isidore of Seville, *Sententiarum,* lib. 3, c. 28 (PL 83, 702): "Tunc amicus amatur, si non pro se, sed pro Deo ametur."

[52] St. Thomas, *De Caritate,* a. 5 ad 2: " . . . caritas in diligendo proximum habet Deum ut rationem formalem objecti . . . "

[53] *Summa Theologica,* II-II, q. 23, a. 5: "charitas est simpliciter una virtus, non distincta in plures species."

aspect . . . Now the aspect under which our neighbor
is loved is God, since what we ought to love in our
neighbor is that he may be in God. Hence, it is
clear that it is specifically the same act whereby we
love God and whereby we love our neighbor. [54]

The love of God is primary, but from this love flows the
love of neighbor;[55] for by our love of God, we love our
neighbor.[56] This fraternal love is but a manifestation of
our love of God, thus if one does not love a neighbor, then
friendship with God is lost.[57] If, however, we love a
neighbor because of some natural motive and not *propter
Deum* then this love pertains to another love—natural love—
and is not charity.[58]

This teaching on the specific unity of charity is clear
both in the writings of St. Gregory the Great[59] and in the
teaching of St. Bonaventure.[60] Love of God leads us to
love all who are objects of God's love and to whom He
communicates an intimate participation in His own proper
life. Thus, all who are capable of friendship with God, all
who are capable of becoming partakers in His Life by
grace, are to be loved, for the sake of God, in charity.[61]

[54] *Ibid.*, II-II, q. 25, a. 1.

[55] St. Isidore of Seville, *Differentiarum*, lib. 2, c. 37, n. 143 (PL
83, 92): "Dilectio in Deum est origo dilectionis in proximum; et
dilectio in proximum cognitio est dilectionis in Deum."

[56] *Ibid.*, *loc. cit.*, " . . . per amorem Dei amor fit proximi."

[57] St. Isidore of Seville, *Sententiarum*, lib. 2, c. 3, n. 7 (PL 83,
603): "Charitas in dilectione Dei et proximi constat. Servat autem
in se dilectionis Dei qui a charitate non dividitur proximi. Qui
a fraterna societate secernitur, a divinae charitatis participatione
privatur."

[58] St. Thomas, *De Caritate*, a. 4: "Sed si diligeremus proximum
ratione sui ipsius, et non ratione Dei, hoc ad aliam dilectionem
pertineret; puta ad dilectionem naturalem . . . "

[59] *Hom. In Evang.*, lib. 2, hom. 26, n. 3 (PL 76, 1199): "Sicut
una est charitas et duo praecepta, ita una spiritus et duo data."

[60] *In III Sent.* dist. 17, a. 1, q. 2 (Quaracchi ed.): " . . . quod duo
sunt praecepta caritatis dicendum quod illa duo praecepta non
sunt diversa formaliter sed solum materialiter, quia unum illorum
clauditur in altero . . . "

[61] St. Thomas, *De Caritate*, a. 7: "Unde diligendus ex caritate

This is supernatural love of neighbor, for we love him and wish him well because of his relation to God. Love of God and neighbor are not two virtues but one supernatural virtue of charity. The fact that we love God either directly in Himself, or indirectly in His image and reflection in our neighbor, does not destroy this specific unity.

Article II

Practice of Love of Neighbor

Love of neighbor, constituted by a supernatural consanguinity and based on divine love, manifests itself in various ways, both in interior affections and in exterior actions. Affective charity comprises all the internal acts which one elicits by means of the infused virtue. This affective love expresses itself in a twofold manner: love of complacence, by which we find joy in our neighbor's possession of supernatural goods, and love of desire, by which we desire that he may receive those supernatural goods which are lacking in his life. Affective charity moves the lover of God and neighbor to effective charity, for charity is manifested by acts proceeding from the virtue.[62] It is not our place here to deal with the interior affections of charity, but it is clear that there is an obligation to love our neighbor with an interior love.[63] Here, we turn our attention to those exterior acts of love inasmuch as they are effects of an efficacious love which is manifested in works.

Deus ut radix beatitudinis; quilibet autem homo debet seipsum ex caritate diligere, ut participet beatitudinem; proximum autem ut socium in participatione beatitudinis." Cf., *Ibid.*, a. 7 ad 17: " . . . cum dicitur aliquis diligere proximum ex caritate haec praepositio *ex* potest designare habitudinem causae finalis, efficientis et formalis. Finalis quidem in quantum dilectio proximi ordinatur ad dilectionem Dei sicut ad finem."

[62] St. Gregory the Great, *Hom. In Ezech.*, lib. 2, hom. 5, n. 6 (PL 76, 988): "Amorem itaque nostrum erga proximum plus bona operatio loquitur quam lingua . . . "

[63] *Cf.* DBU, 1160 where the following propositions were condemned by a Decree of the Holy Office, 2 March, 1671. "Non tenemur proximum diligere actu interno et formali." and 1161 "Praecepta proximum diligendi satisfacere possumus per solos actus externos."

To come to the practice of charity, unless our well-wishing leads us to help our neighbor acquire those goods which he lacks, inasmuch as this is but an exterior effect of an affective love, we do not really love him. These needs can be material or spiritual, which are relieved by the corporal and spiritual works of mercy.[64] After treating of the interior acts or affections of charity, St. Thomas treats of the effective acts of charity, especially those toward a neighbor. Thus, he holds, that beneficence or the "doing good to someone" is the result or effect of interior love.[65] This act of beneficence is not distinct from charity, but is an external expression of this virtue.[66] Chief among the acts of beneficence are the works of almsgiving commanded by charity.

Mercy is that virtue which inclines a man to relieve, out of compassion, the misery of another.[67] In itself, mercy is a moral virtue, but it is the proper effect of charity—for example, "to give alms is an act of charity through the medium of mercy."[68] Mercy leads to acts of beneficence, which has the same formal *ratio* as the object of charity.[69] This act of mercy, coming to the aid of another,[70] is twofold, depending on the nature of the need to be relieved.[71]   St.

[64] Hugh of St. Victor, *De Sacramentis*, lib. 3, p. 13, c. 10 (PL 176, 536): "Quod mandatum [diligendi proximum] tunc profecto implemus si veraciter id quod cupimus nobis bonum, etiam illi cupimus. In quibus enim nosmetipsos recte diligimus proximum nostrum sive ad necessitatem corporis, sive ad animae salutem, sine fictione diligere et quantum rationabiliter adjuvare debemus."

[65] *Summa Theologica*, II-II, q. 31, a. 1.

[66] *Ibid.*, II-II, q. 31, a. 4: "Beneficentia non est aliud virtus a charitate, sed nominat quemdam charitatis actum."

[67] *Cf.*, E. Müller, *Theologia Moralis*, 2, 104.

[68] St. Thomas, *op. cit.*, II-II, q. 32, a. 1: " . . . dare eleemosynam est actus charitatis, misericordia mediante."

[69] *Ibid.*, II-II, q. 31, a. 4: "Eadem autem est ratio formalis objecti charitatis et beneficentiae."

[70] St. Augustine, *De Civitate Dei*, lib. 9, c. 5 (CSEL 40 (1), 415, E. Hoffman): "Quid est autem misericordia, nisi alienae miseriae quaedam in nostro corde compassio, qua utique si possumus subvenire compellimur?"

[71] St. Augustine, *De Moribus Ecclesiae*, lib. 1, c. 27 (PL 32, 1332): "Homo igitur ut homini apparet, anima rationalis est mortali atque

Thomas shows that the distinction of almsdeeds is suitably taken from the various needs which affect either the soul or body of our neighbor, and from the distinction of needs we have the distinction of spiritual and corporal alms.[72]

Since charity does not extend to all things equally, our charity must be ordered.[73] Since the love of charity tends to God as the principle of that love, there must be an order which is regulated ultimately with the first principle of that love, which is God.[74] Charity tends to its objects with an order of precedence and dignity,[75] thus:

> by the order of charity, one is bound to love, after God, (1), oneself with regard to spiritual goods, (2) one's neighbor with regard to the same (spiritual) goods, (3) oneself with regard to bodily goods, (4) one's neighbor with regard to the same (bodily) goods, (5) then oneself and finally one's neighbor with regard to external goods.[76]

When dealing with the acts of beneficence, one must have knowledge of the need and the degree of the need which will serve as directives in the manifestation of charity. Thus, the necessity or need in which we find our neighbor, whether this need be spiritual or temporal, admits of degrees.[77] Since the question of fraternal correction is con-

terreno utens corpore. Partim ergo corpori, partim vero animae hominis benefacit qui proximum diligit."

[72] *Summa Theologica*, II-II, q. 32, a. 2.

[73] St. Augustine, *De Civitate Dei*, lib. 19, c. 14 (CSEL 40 (2), 399 Hoffman).

[74] St. Thomas, *Summa Theologica*, II-II, q. 26, a. 1.

[75] Collegii Salmanticensis, *Cursus Theologicus, de charitate*, (q. 26, disp. 3, dub. 1). 12, 91.

[76] St. Alphonsus, *Theologia Moralis* (ed. Le Noir): "Ordine charitatis quisque tenetur post Deum diligere 1. Seipsum, secundum bona spiritualia. 2, Proximum, quoad eadem bona. 3, Seipsum, quoad bona corporalia. 4, Proximum, quoad eadem. 5, Denique seipsum, et deinde proximum quoad bona externa." I, 319.

[77] T. Iorio, *Theologia Moralis*, "Aliquis ordo charitatis servandus est in dilectione proximi, pro diversitate tum personarum . . . tum conditionum in quibus versantur quaeque variam respicere possunt necessitatem." I, 181.

sidered under the aspect of a spiritual need, we shall here limit ourselves to the consideration of the three grades or degrees of spiritual necessity.

Extreme Spiritual Necessity is present, when, without the aid of others, a man is unable—(physical impossibility)—or is able only with great difficulty—(moral impossibility)[78] to avoid eternal damnation when death is proximate. A non-baptised infant, about to die, is in the circumstance of extreme spiritual necessity. In the case of a man dying in mortal sin who cannot come to his own aid by eliciting an act of perfect contrition, extreme spiritual necessity is present.[79]

Grave Spiritual Necessity is present when one, even though physically and morally capable of saving himself from eternal damnation, finds great difficulty in returning to the love of God without the aid of others. For example, a man would be in grave spiritual necessity if he were a hardened sinner who could help himself, even though there is some difficulty in his return to grace, but will probably not make an act of perfect contrition or will not go to confession by himself unless persuaded to repent by another person.[80]

Common Spiritual Necessity is present when a sinner can easily return to grace without the help of another but will more surely return to the love of God with some outside help, as, for example, by encouragement given him by a friend. Such sinners are placed under the classification of those in common spiritual necessity.[81]

When dealing with these various degrees of spiritual necessity, it can be truly said that, "we love our neighbors as ourselves, when in regard to good conduct and the gain-

[78] F. Cappello, *Tractatus Canonico-Moralis De Sacramentis*, places the notion of moral impossibility, when dealing with spiritual necessity, under the caption *quasi-extrema*. 1, 48.

[79] *Cf.*, St. Alphonsus, *Theologia Moralis* (ed. Le Noir), I, 320. Also *cf.*, E. Genicot, *Theologiae Moralis Institutiones*, I, 192 where the supposition is denied.

[80] *Cf.*, Iorio, *op. cit.*, I, 181.

[81] *Cf.*, B. Merkelbach, *Summa Theologiae Moralis*, I, 694.

ing of eternal salvation, we have concern for their salvation as for our own."[82] However, the degree of necessity being unequal in various circumstances, we have to consider the obligation one has to relieve a neighbor placed in a particular circumstance of spiritual necessity. Theologians are unanimous in their teaching that one has to aid a neighbor, even with the danger of losing his life, when the neighbor is in extreme spiritual necessity. This teaching is clear from Sacred Scripture for "we ought to lay down our lives for the brethren."[83] Even though self-preservation is the first law of nature, when the salvation of one's neighbor is at stake, one is bound to sacrifice bodily life for the spiritual welfare of a neighbor. St. Augustine sees an example of this in the charity of Christ.[84] This sacrifice of bodily life, in the case of an extreme spiritual need, is required by the order of charity, for, even though we must love our body as destined to share in the accidental glory of the beatific vision, our neighbor's soul is far more precious in the eyes of God.[85]

Since the act of coming to a neighbor's aid in extreme spiritual necessity is an act of virtue, due circumstances must be taken into consideration before one would be obliged to give aid when there is question of losing one's own bodily life.[86] One would have to be certain of the neighbor's extreme spiritual necessity; sure that one's aid would be effective; and sure that no one, more bound to give this aid,

---

[82] Julianus Pomerius, *De Vita Contemplativa*, lib. 3, c. 15, n. 3 (PL 59, 477): "Proinde secundum nos proximos diligimus, quando ad mores bonos et ad vitam aeternam consequendam, sicut nobis, saluti eorum consulimus."

[83] 1 John 3:16.

[84] *De Mendacio*, c. 6 (CSEL 41, 426, J. Zycha): "Temporalem plane vitam suam pro aeterna vita proximi non dubitabit christianus amittere; hoc enim praecessit exemplum, ut pro nobis Dominus ipse moreretur."

[85] St. Thomas, *Summa Theologica*, II-II, q. 26, a. 5: "Consociatio in plena participatione beatitudinis, quae est ratio diligendi proximum, est major ratio diligendi quam participatio beatitudinis per redundantiam, quae est ratio diligendi proprium corpus."

[86] *Ibid.*, II-II, q. 33, a. 2: " . . . actus virtutum non quolibet fieri debent, sed observatis debitis circumstantiis . . . "

is willing to give spiritual assistance.[37] Taking the example of the non-baptised infant who is in imminent danger of death, we can see a practical application of these rules. One is sure that the child is in extreme spiritual necessity, for without baptism he cannot enter the kingdom of heaven; death will certainly follow when there is no way to save the child's physical life; one is sure the child can be helped, for, supposing the presence of water, he can easily be baptised. If the pastor of the child were present, he would be more obliged than another because of his office, but if he were unwilling to sacrifice his life, another person, who knows of the need, would be bound by charity to aid the non-baptised child even though there is certainty that he will thereby lose his own bodily life.

One must remember that, even though the neighbor's spiritual necessity be extreme, one would never be allowed to sin in order to bring about the relief of this need.[38] To sin, even venially, is an evil, and, even if done to bring aid to one's neighbor, it is never lawful,[39] for, in the order of charity, one's own spiritual good comes first after God. Even the pagan philosophers recognised this fact, for Cicero holds that it would be against the primary law of friendship to do an evil in order to bring a good to a fellowman.[40] Evil, he holds, is not excused because we do it for a friend.[41]

One would not be bound to come to the aid of a neighbor when he is only in grave spiritual necessity if it would entail the loss of one's bodily life,[42] but aid must be given

---

[37] St. Alphonsus, *Theologia Moralis* (ed. Le Noir): "Tenetur quidem quisque succurrere proximo in extrema necessitate spirituali, adhuc cum jactura suae vitae. Dummodo tria constent: 1, Ut sit aeque spes juvandi . . . 2, Ut proximus nullum alium habeat a quo sublevetur. 3, Ut proximus certo damnatus sit, nisi a te adjuvetur." I, 319.

[38] St. Thomas, *Summa Theologica*, II-II, q. 26, a. 4.

[39] St. Augustine, *op. cit.*, c. 9 (CSEL 41, 433).

[40] *Laelius*, c. 13, n 14: "Haec igitur prima lex amicitiae . . . amicorum causa honesta faciamus." p. 25.

[41] *Ibid*, c. 11, n. 37: "Nulla est igitur excusatio peccati si amici causa peccaveris." p. 22.

[42] St. Alphonsus, *op. cit.*: "Si proximus sit in necessitate tantum gravi non teneris ei succurrere cum periculo vitae, famae vel bonorum nisi sit pastor." I, 319.

him even if there is danger of losing some temporal goods."[93] It is true that, in the order of charity, the spiritual comes before the temporal; but, since a neighbor in grave spiritual necessity can help himself, we would not be bound to sacrifice our bodily life in order to bring him spiritual aid. A pastor of souls, however, would be bound to give this aid in the case of grave spiritual necessity, even though it means grave risk to his bodily life.[94] This obligation of the pastor— an obligation of justice—would come from his office."[95] If, in the case of a private individual, the damage or inconvenience would not be too serious, one would be bound to give this aid.

When there is question of light or common necessity in the spiritual order, one's obligation to aid a neighbor depends on the inconvenience this aid would entail. If one could easily help this neighbor, with little or no inconvenience, one would be bound to give this aid.[96] When dealing with the corporal works of mercy, moral theologians hold that one is bound to give alms from one's superfluities to those in ordinary need.[97] If we are bound to aid materially those in common need, it would seem that we are also bound to give spiritual aid to those in common or light spiritual necessity. This seems to be a valid deduction, for the spiritual works of mercy are superior to the corporal.[98] If one is bound to the lesser, he is also bound to the greater of the same species. Both the corporal and spiritual works of mercy are acts of charity through the medium of mercy. Thus, since one is bound to aid ordinary poor people, one would seem to be bound to aid a neighbor in his light spiritual necessity, if there would be little or no inconvenience in doing so.

---

[93] Merkelbach, *Summa Theologiae Moralis,* "In gravi necessitate spirituali, proximo sucurrendum est, sub gravi, cum aliquo detrimento in bonis temporalibus famae, honoris, fortunae, judicio prudentum aestimando." I, 695.

[94] *Ibid., loc. cit.*

[95] St. Alphonsus, *Theologia Moralis* (ed. Le Noir), I, 319.

[96] Iorio, *Theologia Moralis.* "In communi necessitate utriusque ordinis succurrendum proximo et cum incommodo quidem aliquo, quia id amor proximi exigit.' I, 182.

[97] Merkelbach, *op. cit.,* I, 710.

[98] *Cf.,* St. Thomas, *Summa Theologica,* II-II, q. 32, a. 3.

CHAPTER II

THE PRECEPT OF FRATERNAL CORRECTION

ARTICLE I

NOTION OF FRATERNAL CORRECTION

In order to arrive at a clear concept of fraternal correction, one must study the various definitions given by theologians, for it is by definition that one thing is separated and distinguished from another.[1] Of course, the metaphysical definition, expressing the genus and specific difference of a thing, indicates—in a clear manner by the use of concise terms—the complete essence of the thing to be defined.[2] While various definitions are indicative of the nature of fraternal correction, not all definitions given in manuals of theology are complete. In general, these manuals stress the obligation and its extent rather than the notion itself. Hence, the first purpose of this article will be to point out the most suitable definition, thereby preparing the way for the discussion of the precept, obligation and function of fraternal correction.

By way of clarification, it must be noted that authors use the terms *correctio* and *correptio* interchangeably, although the words differ as to their meaning. Thus, Suarez,[3] Müller,[4] and Lehmkuhl,[5] among others, use the term *fraterna correctio* when dealing with this precept. St. Albert the Great,[6] St. Alphonsus,[7] Billuart[8] and others apply the more technical term *fraterna correptio*. Iorio uses both terms in his definition but in the body of the article treating of the

---

[1] N. Signoriello, *Lexicon Peripateticum Philosophico-Theologicum*, p. 101.

[2] C. Willems, *Institutiones Philosophiae*, I, 75.

[3] F. Suarez, *De Charitate* (disp. 8.). 12, 691.

[4] E. Müller, *Theologia Moralis*, 2, 110.

[5] A. Lehmkuhl, *Theologia Moralis*, I, 422.

[6] St. Albert the Great, *In Evangelium Matthaei* (Matt. 18:15). 20, 674.

[7] St. Alphonsus, *Theologia Moralis* (ed., Le Noir). I, 331.

[8] C. Billuart, *Summa Sancti Thomae*, 3, 535.

definition, he constantly accepts the former.[9] St. Thomas treats of this obligation both in the *Summa Theologica*[10] and in his commentary on the *Sentences*[11] and the more common terminology of *fraterna correctio* is followed. He also has a special tract on fraternal correction.[12] In this dissertation we will follow the more common terminology of fraternal correction.

While the use of the term *correctio* may be the more common, *correptio* or fraternal rebuke is the more technical, in the sense that it refers to an act of charity rather than to the effect of this act. Correction is the result of the act of reprimanding a neighbor. St. Augustine, although he makes use of both terms, [13] in his *De Civitate Dei*[14] follows the more technical terminology of rebuke or reprimand. However, modern theologians use the terms *correctio* and *correptio* interchangeably.

By way of unification, our attention must be given to the definitions and distinctions given in theological tracts. This will aid in establishing a more suitable definition of this obligation of charity. Authors, on the whole, agree as to the existence of this obligation; but the precise nature of the act is expressed in various forms. Perhaps the best way to proceed would be to consider these definitions, in order to bring about a clarified and unified definition of fraternal correction.

St. Thomas proceeds logically by first giving the notion of correction in general and then explains the notion of fraternal correction, by indicating its nature, its motive, and its end. Correction in general is "a remedy which should be used against a man's sin."[15] Following out this general

---

[9] *Theologia Moralis,* I, 190.

[10] II-II, q. 33.

[11] *In IV Sent.* dist. 19 q. 2, a. 1.

[12] *Quaestiones Disputatae de Correctione Fraterna*

[13] *Regula ad Servos Dei,* 7 (PL 32, 1381).

[14] *De Civitate Dei,* lib. 1, c. 9 (CSEL 40 (1), 15 Hoffman).

[15] *Summa Theologica,* II-II, q. 33, a. 1: " . . . correctio delinquentis est quoddam remedium, quod debet adhiberi contra peccatum alicujus."

notion, fraternal correction is "a charitable admonition given to a neighbor to withdraw him from sin."[16]   In this definition of St. Thomas, we have a proper notion of the act, for it is "an admonition" motivated by "fraternal charity" and directed to the spiritual aid of a neighbor so as to withdraw him from sin.   This act of fraternal love is distinguished from judicial correction, primarily by reason of the motive.   For, being moved by fraternal love, one applies fraternal correction to a neighbor's sin in order to bring about his spiritual good, whereas judicial correction attempts to remedy sin inasmuch as it is harmful to a third person or to the common good.[17]

St. Alphonsus defines correction as an admonition by which one tries to withdraw a neighbor from sin.   In the body of this article, he also attaches, to the obligation of fraternal correction, the obligation of forestalling or hindering a neighbor's sin.[18]   Elsewhere,[19] he clearly insists on the obligation of withdrawing a neighbor from the proximate danger of sin.   Lehmkuhl, without a definition of terms, enters immediately into the distinction between fraternal and judicial correction.   He also includes under fraternal correction the duty of forestalling or hindering a neighbor's sin when he is in the proximate danger of grave sin.[20]

Müller defines fraternal correction as an admonition by which one endeavors to withdraw a neighbor from sin and from the proximate occasion of sin.[21]   This definition, although true, does not include a notion of the motive of fraternal correction.   Such a definition is equally applicable

[16] *In* IV *Sent.* dist. 19, q. 2, a. 1:   " . .   admonitio fratris de emendatione delictorum fraterna charitate procedens"

[17] St Thomas, *Summa Theologica*, II-II, q. 33, a. 1:   " . . . in quantum est quoddam malum ipsius peccantis; et ista est proprie fraterna correctio, quae ordinatur ad emendationem delinquentis . . . alia vero correctio est, quae adhibet remedium peccato delinquentis, secundum quod est in malum aliorum, et praecipue in nocumentum communis boni; et talis correctio est actus justitiae, cujus est conservare rectitudinem justitiae unius ad alterum."

[18] *Theologia Moralis* (ed. Le Noir).   I, 331.

[19] *Homo Apostolicus* (tr. 4, c. 2, punct. 3, n. 20).   p. 80.

[20] *Theologia Moralis*, I, 422.

[21] *Theologia Moralis*, 2, 110.

to judicial correction; materially, judicial correction is ordained to the same end as fraternal correction—the removal of sin—but they differ in the fact that these acts of correction proceed from different motives.

Billuart gives a more complete definition, for, when dealing with the notion of fraternal correction, he includes all the distinctive and essential notes. He formulates his definition thus:

> an act of charity and of mercy, by which one strives to turn a neighbor from the evil of sin to the good of virtue by the use of fitting words or by something equivalent.[22]

This exterior act of love of neighbor is properly an act of mercy commanded by charity. Mercy is an interior effect of love[23] which is manifested externally by this act of spiritual almsgiving. The relation between mercy and charity is so intimate that almsgiving, in general, is commonly called charity.[24] Being an act of charity through the medium of mercy, evangelical[25] or fraternal correction can be readily distinguished from judicial correction. Judicial correction is an act of justice; but fraternal correction is directed primarily, not to the good of a third person nor to the common good, but, to the spiritual need of a delinquent. Doing away with sin is procuring a good for a neighbor in sin; and this is an act of charity.[26]

---

[22] *Summa Sancti Thomae:* "Correctio fraterna est actus charitatis et misericordiae, quo per convenientem sermonem, vel aliquid aequivalens, proximum a malo peccati ad bonum virtutis convertere nitimur." 3, 536.

[23] St. Thomas, *Summa Theologica*, II-II, q. 28.

[24] P. Abelard, *Sermones et Opuscula Ascetica*, sermo 30 (PL 178, 565): "Cum autem charitas in Deum ferveat semper, maxime illa fervere cognoscitur quae per compassionem fraternam in eleemosynis exhibetur. Unde et per excellentiam quamdam ipsa eleemosynae largitas quasi proprio jam vel speciali nomine charitas vocari consuevit."

[25] A. Reiffenstuel, *Jus Canonicum*, 6, 100.

[26] St. Thomas, *De Correctione Fraterna*, a. 1: "Et quia carere malo habet rationem boni . . . inde est, quod ad rationem dilectionis pertinet, ut etiam velimus mala dilectis nostris non inesse . . . etiam

Billuart, in his definition, does not restrict the means of correction to verbal rebuke, as some do,[27] but includes any means which would be "equivalent" to words in bringing about the desired end. Our Lord used verbal rebuke;[28] but the gospel gives a striking example of the "something equivalent" for after the threefold denial of Peter, " . . . the Lord turned and looked upon Peter. And Peter remembered the word of the Lord . . . and went out and wept bitterly."[29]

This act of love must be regulated and directed by the virtue of prudence.[30] This is pointed out in the definition of Billuart by the use of the terms *per convenientem sermonem.* The reason for the exercise of prudence in this act of fraternal love is evident. We seek the conversion of our neighbor from the evil of sin to the good of virtue. Prudence, however, directs the ways and means by which his particular fault is to be corrected and by which his correction is to be sought, for prudence gives the right direction of means to a particular end.[31]

While the definition of Billuart does not include the notion of preventing sin when one's neighbor is in the proximate occasion of sin, in the body of this article he holds that rebuke or correction properly refers to sins committed; but it also can be extended to the prevention of those sins which are likely to be committed soon. This prevention of sin is an act of spiritual alms, whether it be called correction, monition, counsel, or instruction.[32]

ad rationem dilectionis pertinet, ut ad amicos bona operemur, et mala eorum impediamus."

[27] H. Serra, *Memoriale Theologiae Moralis,* p. 109.

[28] Luke 19:45-46.

[29] Luke 22:61-62.

[30] St. Thomas, *Summa Theologica,* II-II, q. 33, a. 2 ad 2: " . . . talis admonitio [fratris] principaliter est actus charitatis quasi imperantis, prudentiae vero secundario quasi exsequentis, et dirigentis actum."

[31] *Ibid., loc. cit.* " . . . prudentia facit rectitudinem in his quae sunt ad finem . . . admonitio quae fit in correctione fraterna . . . est actus . . . prudentiae vero secundario quasi exsequentis, et dirigentis actum."

[32] Billuart, *Summa Sancti Thomae,* " . . . quamvis . . . correctio proprie respiciat peccatum commissum, conveniunt tamen omnes

Although all these definitions of the authors are in substantial agreement, some include notes not found in others. Hence, we shall attempt to form a definition from various authors. In this way we shall have a composite, but unified, definition of the term under consideration. Of course, some notes of this proposed definition will be subject to a more technical treatment in the analysis of the chapter on the subject and object of fraternal correction.[33]

Fraternal rebuke or corection may be defined as:

> any prudent word or deed, springing from the virtues of charity and mercy, by which one prudently attempts to procure a neighbor's personal spiritual good by turning him from sin and from the proximate occasion of sin.

This definition gives an adequate notion of fraternal correction, for all the essential properties of the act are clearly indicated. These essential properties may be outlined here:

1) Fraternal correction is an act of charity through the medium of mercy and directed by the virtue of prudence.

2) The end proposed by this charitable act is the personal spiritual good of a neighbor to be procured, by turning him to the good of virtue.

3) The end proposed can be attained by word or deed. The means to this charitable end are not restricted except by the direction of prudence.

4) Since the absence of evil is a good, this act of charity can be twofold: the turning of a neighbor away from sins already committed and the preventing of sin in the future when our neighbor is in the proximate occasion of sin.

parem obligationem esse impediendi peccatum futurum imminens, quia est pariter eleemosyna spiritualis, et sive dicatur correptio, sive monitio, sive instructio, sive consilium, perinde est." 3, 536.

[33] *Cf., infra,* Chapter 3.

ARTICLE II

BASIS OF THE OBLIGATION OF FRATERNAL CORRECTION

Theologians, while differing in their explanation and extension of the precept of fraternal correction, are all in agreement that this precept is of natural law. Our task, here, is not to prove the existence of a natural law; nevertheless, in order to see the application of this law in our study, we must consider the formal nature of this law. In this way, a proper application can be made relative to this particular precept.

Some assert that rational nature itself, inasmuch as it is the basis of good and evil in human actions, is the natural law.[34] Thus, actions are good or bad depending on their conformity or non-conformity with rational nature. Hence, if we follow this opinion, in order that fraternal correction be a good act, it would have to be in agreement with rational nature and the omission would be an evil because of the inherent discord with nature. However, for St. Thomas, natural reason is the power which determines good and bad actions.[35] This, perhaps, bears out the text of St. Paul,[36] for it is by the light of natural reason that a man knows what must be done and what must be avoided.[37]

Law, in general, may be viewed actively and passively; actively, as existing in the mind and will of the legislator; passively, as made known to the subjects of the law. On the part of the Legislator, God, the eternal law is "nothing else than the Divine Wisdom directing all actions and movements."[38] On the part of rational creatures, the subject, the

---

[34] G. Vasquez, *Commentariorum ac Disputationum in Primam Secundae Sancti Thomae*, 2, 4-5.

[35] *Summa Theologica*, I-II, q. 100, a. 1.

[36] Romans 2:14-15: "When the Gentiles who have no law do by nature what the Law prescribes, these having no law are a law unto themselves. They show the works of the Law written in their hearts."

[37] *Summa Theologica*, I-II, q. 91, a. 2: ". . . lumen rationis naturalis quo discernimus quid sit bonum, et quid sit malum, quod pertinet ad naturalem legem . . . "

[38] *Ibid.*, I-II, q. 93 ,a. 1: ". . . lex aeterna nihil aliud est, quam ratio divinae sapientiae, secundum quod est directiva omnium actuum et motionum."

natural law is his participation in the eternal law of God.[39] The supreme norm of morality, then, is the eternal law, but the proximate rule is right reason whereby rational creatures determine what is good or what is bad.[40] The dictates of the natural law are founded on the first principles of practical reason, namely good is to be done and evil is to be avoided; upon this principle, all principles of the natural law are founded.[41]

From the first principle of natural law, it is clearly evident that love of God is a precept of this law. The will naturally goes out to good; and God is the Absolute Good and thus must be loved.[42] This fact led Berti[43] to consider the love of God as the first principle of natural law. Love of neighbor is also a principle of natural law. This fact can be proved from the likeness or similarity between men in the natural order. St. Thomas bases this natural precept of love of neighbor on the fact that men are like each other[44] and this likeness is the foundation of the natural precept of love of neighbor, for:

> likeness properly speaking is the cause of love . . . for the very fact that two men are alike, having as it were one form, makes them to be, in some way, one in that form . . . Hence the affections of one tend to the other, as being one with him; and he wishes him good as to himself.[45]

It might be asked what is the cause of love? We have already indicated that likeness is the cause of love, but the

[39] *Ibid.*, I-II, q. 91, a. 2: " . . . lex naturalis nihil aliud est, quam participatio legis aeternae in rationali creatura."

[40] *Ibid., loc. cit.*

[41] St. Thomas, *op. cit.*, I-II, q. 94, a. 2: "Hoc est ergo primum praeceptum legis, quod bonum est faciendum et prosequendum, et malum vitandum; et super hoc fundantur omnia alia praecepta legis naturae . . . "

[42] St. Thomas, *Quodlibetales*, 1, a. 8.

[43] *Cf.*, Merkelbach, *Summa Theologiae Moralis*, I, 231, fn. 1.

[44] *In Duo Praecepta Caritatis Et In Decem Legis Praecepta Expositio*, opus 3, c. 7.

[45] St. Thomas, *Summa Theologica*, I-II, q. 27, a. 3.

fundamental motive of love is *good* in general, for "to love
is to will good for some one."[46]   The Angelic Doctor defines
love, in general, as "the first movement of the will or any
appetite."[47]   Goodness by its very nature is lovable and
love by its very nature is directed to good.   In the natural
love of rational creatures, who have the power to discern
good, the will goes out to another because of goodness.   Thus,
the will is directed to good simply and natural love of neighbor is directed to a fellowman because of his goodness.   Man,
having the power to discern good in things, regards other rational creatures as good simply.   In the "love" we have for
things around us, as, for example, "love" of wine, we do
not love them simply but only in as far as they are good for
us, but when our love is directed to another rational creature
we love him for his goodness, for, taken simply, loving
another for his goodness is love simply.[48]   Since the love of
another—love of friendship—is a principle of activity, love
manifests itself by its proper effects, and the first of these
effects is benevolence.[49]   When we correct a neighbor, we
love a neighbor.   Loving and willing good, we must take
the practical means to activate our benevolent love.

The concept of correction, as an expression of love, is not
something developed out of christianity for we find mention
of it in the pre-christian pagan philosophers.   Cicero is explicit in his statement that the giving and receiving of
advice is a characteristic of true friendship,[50] and, like
Aristotle,[51] recognized correction as a sign of love.[52]

St. Thomas, in treating of this obligation, holds that all
precepts dealing with the rendering of service to a neighbor

---

[46] *Ibid.*, I-II, q. 26, a. 4:   " . . . amare est velle alicui bonum . . . "

[47] *Ibid.*, I, q. 20, a. 1:   "Primus enim motus voluntatis et
cujuslibet appetitivae virtutis est amor."

[48] *Cf.*, St. Thomas, *In X Libros Ethicorum ad Nicomachum*, lib.
9, lect. 4-5.

[49] *Ibid.*, lib. 9, lect. 5.

[50] *Laelius*, c. 25, n. 21:   "Ut igitur monere et moneri proprium
est verae amicitiae."   [49].

[51] *Nicomachan Ethics*, bk. 9 ch. 13, n. 1165b (ed. R. McKeon).
p. 1080.

[52] *Laelius* (c 13, n. 44.).   p. 25.

are reduced to the Fourth Commandment[53] for the obligation to give alms and the precept of honoring parents are
reduced to the same law, while, by the name *parent* all
neighbors are to be understood.[54] St. Albert the Great places
the obligation of spiritual almsgiving, which includes fraternal correction, under the same precept.[55]

Although charity includes man's natural love of God, as
well as his love of fellowman, here we deal only with the
obligation of fraternal correction as an obligation arising
from supernatural fellowship known by faith. The motive
of our correction is not alone man's likeness to us or the
closeness of natural bonds, as known by the light of reason,
but primarily man's likeness to us, in the supernatural
order, as known by the light of faith. We have seen that the
act of love of God and neighbor, which we call charity, is
supernatural in its very essence and thus we love God and
neighbor for the sake of the lovableness of the Absolute
Good. That there is an obligation of supernatural love of
neighbor is stated above.

When one's attention is turned to the supernatural love of
neighbor, whatever is a necessary condition of that love is
a matter of precept. Love, being an act of the will by which
one wishes well to another, "carries into effect, if possible,
the thing it wills . . . the result of an act of love is that man
is beneficent to his friend."[56] Now this necessity of willing
the means to our love of neighbor is clear, for:

> as love of neighbor is a matter of precept, whatever
> is a necessary condition to love our neighbor is also
> a matter of precept. Now the love of neighbor re-
> quires that we should not only be well-wishers of our
> neighbor but also his well-doers, according to 1 Jn.
> 3:18, 'Let us not love in word, neither with the
> tongue but in deed and in truth.'[57]

[53] *Summa Theologica*, II-II, q. 33, a. 2 ad 2.
[54] *In IV Sent.* dist. 15, q. 2, a. 1.
[55] *In IV Sent.* (dist. 15, a. 16.). 29, 495.
[56] St. Thomas, *Summa Theologica*, II-II, q. 31, a. 1: "Voluntas
autem est effectiva eorum, quae vult, si facultas adsit .. .benefacere
amico ex actu dilectionis consequitur."
[57] *Ibid.*, II-II, q. 32, a. 5.

If, when an occasion arises, we are able to help a neighbor and yet fail to do so, we do not "love-in-deed." This "love-in-deed" is a means to our supernatural love of neighbor and thus a precept of the divine law. Naturally man corrects a neighbor because man loves good; supernaturally, a man corrects his neighbor—as made known by the light of faith—because of a direct reference to a supernatural good. Since particular details of the natural law are often difficult to deduce with certainty from the general principles, a divine positive precept of fraternal correction was called for .[58] Moreover, it was God's will that this obligation of love be fulfilled through the supernatural motive of charity. This positive precept is found both in the Old[59] and New Law[60] but we shall follow the law as stated by St. Matthew. This text of St. Matthew is used by all the theologians in their explanation of the obligation.

In the Gospel according to St. Matthew we read:

> But if thy brother sin against thee, go and show him his fault, between thee and him alone. If he listen to thee, thou hast won thy brother. But if he do not listen to thee, take with thee one or two more so that on the word of two or three witnesses every word may be confirmed. And if he refuse to hear them, appeal to the Church, but if he refuse to hear even the Church, let him be to thee as the heathen and publican.[61]

This text will be treated in detail in the next chapter, for it is the basis of the various distinctions made by the theologians. While all accept this text as fundamental to the positive precept of fraternal correction, various interpretations of the text have led to different opinions and explanations of the obligation, both with regard to the subject and its object.

[58] *Cf.*, St. Thomas, *Summa Theologica*, I-II, q. 91, a. 4.
[59] Proverbs 27:5, Ecclesiasticus 19:14, Psalm 140:5, Leviticus 19:17.
[60] Matthew 18:15-17, Luke 17:3, James 5:19.
[61] Matthew 18:15-17.

The teaching of the Fathers of the Church on the obligation of fraternal correction is clearly stated. St. Augustine holds that the omission of correction makes one worse than the delinquent.[62] Comparing the spiritual and corporal works of mercy, St. John Chrysostom makes use of the parable of the unfaithful servant in his teaching on fraternal correction. The fact that we are not dealing with temporal needs of a neighbor but with the very life of his soul, leads St. John Chrysostom to conclude that the punishment of the one who does not correct a neighbor will be far greater than that meted out to the unfaithful servant in the parable.[63] St. Basil the Great states that one cannot be silent when another sins, but rather he is bound to carry out the injunction of the Lord as stated in the Gospel of St. Matthew.[64] The teaching of other Fathers and early ecclesiastical writers will be shown throughout the following chapters.

Basing his teaching on the general obligation of love of neighbor, St. Thomas, in addition to the teaching of the *Summa Theologica*,[65] wrote a special treatise to prove that there is an obligation to correct a neighbor.[66] Gregory of Valentia holds that the precept of fraternal correction is certain *ex fide*,[67] while Suarez maintains that it would be heresy to deny the existence of the precept and close to heresy to hold that this precept is not contained in the cited passages of Sacred Scripture.[68] Natalis Alexander points out that one cannot fulfill the precept of love of neighbor

---

[62] *De Verbis Domini,* serm. 82, c. 4, n. 7 (PL 38, 508-509).

[63] *Hom. In Epist. ad Hebraeos,* c. 12, hom. 30 (PG 63, 211-212).

[64] *Moralia,* Reg. 52, c. 2 (PG 31, 788).

[65] *Summa Theologica,* II-II, q. 33, a. 1.

[66] *Quaestiones Disputatae de Correctione Fraterna,* a. 1: " . . . ideo tenetur homo ex praecepto dilectionis ut proximo auxilium ferat ad virtutem consequendam, dando ei consilium et auxilium ad bene agendum . . . "

[67] *Commentaria Theologica, de charitate,* q. 10, punct. 2: "Ex fide certissimum est, correctionem fraternam non modo utilem esse, sed etiam necessaria(m), divino praecepto obliga(n)te sub peccato mortali." 3, 806.

[68] *De Charitate,* disp. 8, sect. 1, n. 3. "Dico simpliciter esse hereticum negare illud [praeceptum de correctione fraterna], et fere hereticum negare contineri in citatis locis Scripturae." 12, 693

unless one tries to lead a neighbor to God, offering him those things which are necessary for this end; fraternal correction is but one of the many means to this end.[69] Commenting on the passage from the Old Law, [70] "Reprove thy neighbor . . . ," De Coninck shows that this is not a mere counsel but a true precept and he cites the text of St. Matthew in proof of this statement.[71] Wiggers also bases the obligation of fraternal correction on this text of St. Matthew, showing that this act of fraternal correction flows from the very nature of love.[72]

While the law of fraternal correction is not contained in the New Code of Canon Law, it did have a place in the former law of the Church.

> Both priests and all the rest of the faithful should have great concern for those who perish, so that by their reproof they may either correct their ways, or if they are incorrigible, cut them off from the Church.[73]

The fact that a gloss would have us understand *fideles* in the sense of prelate does not militate against the force of this law.[74] St. Thomas used this text to show that the faithful, and not only prelates, were bound by the law of fraternal correction.[75] Gregory of Valentia[76] and others used this same text in pointing out the ecclesiastical law of fraternal

---

[69] *Theologia Dogmatica et Moralis*, 2, 469.

[70] Ecclesiasticus 19:14.

[71] *De Moralitate, Natura Et Effectibus Actuum Supernaturalium In Genere, Et Fide, Spe, ac Charitate Speciatim*, (lib. 4, disp. 28. dub. 2). p. 568.

[72] *Commentaria De Virtutibus Theologicis, Fide, Spe, Charitate*, p. 305.

[73] *Decretum Gratiani*, c. 14, C. XXIV, q. 3: "Tam sacerdotes quam reliqui fideles omnes summam curam habere debent de his qui pereunt; quatenus eorum redargatione, aut corrigantur a peccatis, aut si incorrigibiles apparuerint, ab ecclesia separentur." 3, 1680.

[74] *Ibid., Glos.* "[Fideles] id est praelati." 3, 1679.

[75] *Summa Theologica*, II-II, q. 33, a. 3.

[76] *Commentaria Theologica, de charitate* (q. 10, punct. 1). 3, 808.

correction, as applied to the faithful. However, since this law is not contained in the New Code of Canon Law, the faithful are no longer bound by ecclesiastical law to correct another, but this correction remains a prescription of the natural and positive divine law.[77] Judicial reprimand has a place in the New Code,[78] and correction is listed as one of the penal remedies for crime.[79] Among the obligations listed for a Dean—*vicarius foraneus*—the Code states that he has an obligation to watch over the actions of the clergy to see that they fulfill their obligations,[80] and he is to make a report to the Bishop of any scandals that have arisen. The pastor is also instructed to watch over the faith and morals of his people,[81] and this would include a reprimand for faults committed. These obligations of correction and remedies for crime arise from the office of Bishop, Dean, and Pastor, and thus they pertain to judicial correction rather than to fraternal correction.

[77] *Cf., Can.* 6, nr. 6.
[78] *Can.* 1947-1953.
[79] *Can.* 2306.
[80] *Can.* 447, nr. 1.
[81] *Can.* 469.

CHAPTER III

OBLIGATION OF FRATERNAL CORRECTION

Introduction

One of the chief characteristics of law is its binding force. A law, being the measure of moral acts with respect to their goodness and rectitude, impels one to perform the prescribed actions.[1] Thus far, we have explained the general notions of charity and the application of these notions to love of neighbor. A primary consideration led to the conclusion that one must aid a neighbor in need, whether the need be of a temporal or of a spiritual nature. Under the consideration of a spiritual need, fraternal correction was established as a precept.

There are various types of law; one regulating the performance of an act, so that the prescribed action is of obligation, as in the case of almsgiving; other laws, although not requiring the performance of an act, require that, if the act be placed, a particular mode of execution be observed, as, for example, the law to pray attentively. This precept, although not rendering the act of prayer obligatory (though it is obligatory in virtue of another precept), does impose an obligation so that, if one prays, one must pray with attention.[2]

When dealing with the precept of fraternal correction, both these aspects—one regulating the performance of the act and the other regulating the mode of execution—must be considered. The obligatory aspect of the precept has already been established, but now our attention must be turned to the extent and to the gravity of this precept. The precept of fraternal correction is an affirmative precept,[3] binding only in certain circumstances.[4] Therefore, the con-

---

[1] Suarez, *De Legibus ac Legislatore Deo*, (lib. 1, c. 1, n. 7). 5, 2-3.

[2] *Ibid.*, (lib. 1, c. 1, c. 1, n. 8). 5,3.

[3] St Thomas, *Summa Theologica*, II-II, q. 33, a. 2.

[4] St. Thomas, *De Correctione Fraterna*, a. 1: " . . . correctio fraterna sub praecepto cadit secundum debitas circumstantias, secundum quod est actus virtutis."

32

ditions necessary for the precept to be of obligation and the causes excusing one, in a particular case, from this obligation are of great importance in the treatment of this question of correction. The extent of the obligation will be treated in a twofold manner; first, with reference to those who are bound to give correction; and secondly, with reference to those to whom this correction should be given. If, when the requisite conditions are present, one gives correction, then, the manner of correction plays a role of significance in the fulfillment of this obligation. The object of correction or its subject matter will entail a consideration of the threefold classification of sin: mortal, venial and material.

These considerations are based chiefly on the proper understanding of the text of St. Matthew: "But if thy brother sin against thee, go and show him his fault, between thee and him alone . . . "[5]

A—Subject

Article I

THE EXTENT OF THE OBLIGATION

The precept of fraternal correction is imposed on all men as an obligation binding in conscience. This is the unanimous teaching of theologians as is evidenced by the teaching of St. Bonaventure,[6] Sylvester,[7] Navarrus,[8] Gregory of Valentia,[9] Suarez[10] and St. Alphonsus[11] to mention only a few. St. Thomas states that the correction "which seeks in a special way to recover an erring brother by means of a

---

[5] Matthew 18:15.

[6] *Speculum Conscientiae*, (c. 3, 29). 8, 639.

[7] Sylvester Prierias (Mazzolini), *Summa Summarum*, I, 163.

[8] Navarrus (Martin Azpilcueta), *Enchiridion, Sive Manuale Confessariorum et Poenitentium*, (c. 4, n. 12). I, 440.

[9] *Commentaria Theologica, de charitate*, (q. 10, punct. 3). 3, 823.

[10] *De Charitate*, (disp. 8, sect. 4, n. 3). 12, 698.

[11] *Theologia Moralis* (ed. Le Noir) I, 332.

simple warning . . . pertains to anyone who has charity,"[12] Cajetan[13] and Bannes[14], commenting on this text, understand St. Thomas to refer to all men. It is certain that this phase "to anyone who has charity" is not to be understood in the restrictive sense so that only those in sanctifying grace would be bound to correct; but it is to be taken in the universal sense of those who are bound by the law of charity, whether they actually possess charity or not. This conclusion will be confirmed later in this article when we treat the question of the sinner's obligation to correct.

The universality of the obligation of fraternal correction is clearly expressed in St. Augustine's *On the City of God*, for, as the Saint asserts, even though the one correcting is not the delinquent's superior, one is still bound to correct.[15] The reason for the universality of the precept, obliging as it does all men, is indicated in Sacred Scripture for God "gave to every one of them a commandment concerning his neighbor."[16] St. Augustine, when dealing with the general obligation of correction, distinguished it from that correction given by a superior: the superior is bound more than others, for his is a twofold duty: one of charity and the other of justice.[17]

Since the precept of fraternal correction is of natural law, it follows that all men, without exception, are bound to correct a delinquent neighbor; for all men are subject to the natural law. It is indeed true that this particular

[12] *Summa Theologica*, II-II, q. 33, a. 3; "Quae [correctio] specialiter tendit ad emendationem fratris delinquentis per simplicem admonitionem . . . pertinet ad quemlibet charitatem habentem . . . "

[13] *Commentaria in Summa Theologicam S. Thomas Aquinatis* (in Leonine ed., of the *Opera Omnia* of St. Thomas.). *In* II-II, q. 33, a. 2:" Per ly *charitatem habentem* intelligas omnem hominem habentem, vel in actu vel in potentia: alioquin, si de habente illam in actu solum intelligeretur, nullus tenebit se obligatum ad correctionem fraternam; quoniam nullus scit, se habere actualiter charitatem."

[14] *De Fide, Spe et Charitate*, (q. 33, a. 3). p. 870.

[15] *De Civitate Dei*, lib. 1, c. 9, n. 3 (CSEL 40 (1), 17-18 Hoffman).

[16] Ecclesiasticus 17: 12.

[17] *Op. cit., loc. cit.*

precept is a remote conclusion from the first principles of natural law; but if men know of this obligation—*in actu secundo*—they are bound by its prescriptions. The Evangelical Law of fraternal correction does not differ from the precept as found in the natural law, save in its motive, which is supernatural.[18] The obligation of charity, love of God and neighbor, being universal, the obligations which arise from this law of supernatural love are also universal. Hence, since the obligation of giving aid to a neighbor in need, whether the need be of a temporal or a spiritual nature, arises from the general obligation of love, it follows that this deed of love is universal in the extent of its obligation.[19] Certainly, the charitable act of correction pertains to all men.[20] Christ, in the text of St. Matthew, uses the term *brother;* and all men are brothers by their common participation in human nature,[21] and all men are brothers in the supernatural order—a unity based on the common destiny of union with God for all eternity.

A special difficulty is present when one deals with the obligation enjoined upon a sinner who has to correct another delinquent. It is the common teaching of theologians that the sinner is not released from the obligation of correcting another sinner. Thus, Navarrus,[22] Gregory of Valentia,[23] Cajetan,[24] Bannez,[25] and Daelman[26] hold that the sinner is bound by this obligation of charitable correction. Suarez maintains that a sinner is apt to give correction and, given

---

[18] Suarez, *De Religione* (lib. 10, c. 7, n. 14). 14, 1095.

[19] Gregory of Valentia, *op. cit., de charitate* (q. 9, punct. 1). 3, 757.

[20] St. Thomas, *De Correctione Fraterna*, a. 1 ad 17: " . . . correctio caritativa est officium omnium."

[21] Gregory of Valentia, *op. cit., de charitate* (q. 10, punct. 3). 3, 823.

[22] *Enchiridion, Sive Manuale*, c. 24, n. 12: "Fraterna correctio una de septem eleemosynis spiritualibus . . . ad q[uam] praecepto naturali o[mn]es et et[iam] subditi, justi et peccatores." I, 140.

[23] *Op. cit., de charitate* (q. 10, punct. 3). 3, 823.

[24] *Comm. In* II-II, q. 33, a.. 3.

[25] *De Fide, Spe et Charitate* (q. 33, a. 3). p. 870.

[26] *Theologia, seu Observationes Theologicae In Summam D. Thomae, de fide spe et charitate* (q. 9, obs. 11). 4, 311.

the necessary conditions, he is obliged to correct.[27]   The position of St. Thomas, taken in the light of his commentators, would not exempt the sinner from this obligation. He holds that *all having charity* are capable of giving correction but this seems to mean that all who are bound by the law of charity, i. e. all men, are bound to give correction.[28]

Elsewhere, it is true that St. Thomas might seem to exclude the sinner from this obligation, in the sense that a sinner's state of soul proves somewhat of a hindrance to this act of love. He gives three reasons for this statement:

> First, because of previous sin, a sinner is unworthy to correct another; especially if he has committed a greater sin, he is not worthy to correct another for lesser sins.

> Second, because of the scandal which results from this correction, such correction is shameful, if the corrector's sin is manifest; for it would seem that he who corrects, does not correct out of charity, but more for show . . .

> Third, because of the corrector's pride . . . thinking his own sins light, he sets himself above his neighbor in his own estimation, judging his neighbor's sin with severity, as though he were a just man.[29]

For these reasons, St. Thomas indicates that a sinner would be less worthy to correct another; but if the sinner reprove or correct another delinquent with humility, he would not sin.[30] Fraternal correction, rightly understood and carried out with love, does not imply superiority over others. This passage of St. Thomas' *Summa* is not meant to release the

[27] *De Charitate* (disp. 8, sect. 1, n. 6). 12, 699.

[28] *Summa Theologica*, II-II, q. 33, a. 3. Cf., Cajetan and Bannez, *Comm. in loc. cit.*

[29] *Summa Theologica*, II-II, q. 33, a. 5.

[30] *Ibid., loc. cit.*: "Si peccator cum humilitate corripiat delinquentem, non peccat, nec sibi novam condemnationem acquirit." Cf., *De Correctione Fraterna*, a. 1 ad 15.

sinner from the obligation of correction, for the Angelic Doctor is pointing out that the sinner should not correct another in a bad spirit, that is with vanity and pride. He is dealing, not with the cessation of the obligation for a sinner, but rather with the perverse and proud correction given by some.[31] Sin does not necessarily destroy the good of nature; it does not deprive man of his good judgment; hence, even the sinner is competent and obliged to correct.[32]

St. Augustine, in his work *De Catechizandis Rudibus*, shows that the works of mercy are profitable for the sinner for:

> If sadness seize us because of some error or sin of our own, let us not only remember that an afflicted spirit is a sacrifice to God (Ps. 50:19) but also the words "for as a water quenches a flaming fire, so also almsgiving quenches sin," (Eccles. 3:33) and "for I desire," he says, "mercy rather than sacrifice." (Osse 6:6) . . . thus if some fire of sin has arisen from our concupiscence, and we are troubled on account of this, let us rejoice in the opportunity to perform a most merciful act . . . Moreover, were it only profitable to do this, but not harmful to leave it undone, it would be unfortunate to reject the offered remedy in the danger of our neighbor's and our own salvation . . . what foolishness it is, when our sin pains us, to want to sin again by not giving the Lord's money to those who desire and ask for it.[33]

Admittedly, this text does not deal specifically with the matter of fraternal correction. However, since correction is the more commendable of the spiritual works of mercy,[34]

---

[31] Gregory of Valentia, *Commentaria Theologica, de charitate*, q. 10, punct. 3: "Non enim vult S. Thomas significare, quod propter has causas non debet peccator ullo modo corripere proximum, quasi jam idcirco liber fit a corripiendi obligatione: sed quod non debeat corripere modo pravo et perverso." 3, 824.

[32] Billuart, *Summa Sancti Thomae*, 3, 541.

[33] *De Catechizandis Rudibus*, c. 14, n. 22 (PL 40, 327).

[34] Salmanticensis Collegii, *Cursus Theologicus, arbor praedica-*

this text may be used to prove that correction is not only profitable for the sinner but also that it is of obligation, so that to omit it would be sinful.

Cajetan[35] and Daelman,[36] rather than releasing the sinner from this obligation, show that it is most profitable for him to correct. If the sinner were free from this obligation, then sin would be a reason for not keeping the divine precepts. This certainly is false doctrine.[37] Even though a man be in the state of sin, he is still bound by the law of God; and he must take the necessary means to fulfill the law, even if the state of grace is required for its proper fulfillment. In general, a law can be fulfilled even though a person be in the state of sin. Baius was in error on this point.[38] Since the law of fraternal correction is intended primarily for our neighbor's spiritual good, the substance of the act—the reprimand or correction—can be fulfilled even though a man is not in the state of grace.[39] Whether or not the sinner has an obligation to return to grace in order to correct another, as some hold, will be a subject treated in the next article.

Various texts from Sacred Scripture and from the writings of the Fathers could be advanced against the conclusion that a sinner is also bound to correct his neighbor. Thus, we read: "to the sinner God hath said: 'Why dost thou declare my justice and take my covenant in thy mouth?'."[40] But this does not release the sinner from the

---

mentalis, n. 26: "Inter spirituales eleemosynas celebrior est corrigere peccantem." 5, 430.

[35] *Comm* in II-II, q. 33, a. 5

[36] *De Charitate* (obs. 10). 4, 311.

[37] Navarrus, *Enchiridion, Sive Manuale* (c. 24, n. 12). I, 140

[38] DBU, 1016: "Non est vera legis oboedientia quae fit sine charitate."

[39] Gregory of Valentia, *op cit., de charitate*, q. 10, punct. 3: "Peccator . . . potest nihilominus modo dicto [amota suspicione superbiae et vanitatis, temperantaque sua indignitate per humilitatem] implere id praeceptum quoad substantiam actus: id quod satis est ut vitetur novum peccatum contra illud praeceptum." 3, 824-825.

[40] Psalm 49:16.

obligation of correction, for God here reprimands "the hypocritical sinners who repeat His Law and His Commandments while setting them at variance by their conduct."[41] Our Lord also reprimanded this type of correction when He said: "Thou hypocrite, first cast out the beam from thy own eye, and then thou wilt see clearly to cast out the speck from thy brother's eye."[42] St. Jerome interprets these words in the sense that our Lord "is speaking to those who, while guilty themselves of mortal sin, have no patience with the lesser sins of their neighbor."[43] In a work attributed to St. John Chrysostom we read that this is a protest against the sinner, who, while claiming that his motive for correction is his neighbor's salvation, in reality wishes to hide his own sin by good teaching and thus be praised by men.[44] Hence, St. John Chrysostom teaches that:

the precept, then, in these words is that he who is subject to countless vices should not be a severe judge of another's sin, especially if they are venial: it does not forbid reproof or correction, but it does forbid one to neglect his own sins and to scoff at the sins of others.[45]

It is true that St. Augustine holds that it is the duty of good and benevolent men to reprove the faults of others,[46] but this does not mean that a sinner is not obliged to correct another. The whole context deals rather with the sinner correcting in a spirit of humility, for:

When necessity compels us to censure or rebuke someone, first let us recall whether or not we were ever guilty of this sin . . . and if we were never

[41] J. Fillion, *The New Psalter of the Roman Breviary*, (In Ps. 49:16). p. 244.

[42] Matthew 7:3.

[43] *Commentarium in Evangelium Matthaei*, lib. 1. c. 7 (PL 26, 46-47): "De his loquitur, qui cum ipsi mortali crimine teneantur obnoxii, minora peccata fratribus non concedunt."

[44] Cf., St. Thomas, *Summa Theologica*, II-II, q. 33, a. 5.

[45] *Hom. in Matt*, hom. 23 (PG 57, 310).

[46] *De Sermone Domini in Monte*, lib. 2, c. 19, n. 64 (PL 34, 1298).

guilty, let us remember that we are men and could
have been guilty of it: if we had it once on our
conscience but have it no longer, our common weakness touches our minds so that mercy and not hate
precede that correction or censure . . . But if we find
that we are guilty of the same sin . . . we must not
chide or reprove him; but let us lament, and let
us invite him, not to conform to our actions but to
repent with us.[47]

St. Thomas, commenting on this text of St. Augustine, concludes that "if a sinner reproves a delinquent, with humility he will not sin."[48] St. Isidore of Seville holds that "he
who is subject to vice should not correct the vices of
others."[49] Again, this text is to be understood in the sense
that a sinner is not to correct in a perverse and arrogant
spirit. These, and similar texts, do not signify that a sinner
is released from the obligation of giving correction but
they rather indicate that he is not to correct in a spirit of
pride. The *beam* can be cast out by humility; for when a
man acknowledges his own fault, he is not a hypocrite and
he can lead others to virtue, not as one commanding, but by
inviting others to repent with him.[50]

While all men are bound to carry out this act of love,
superiors and parents have a greater obligation than others
to correct a delinquent subject,[51] for they have a double
obligation—charity and justice or piety— of correcting. St.
Augustine, commenting on the words of the Prophet Eze-

---

[47] *Ibid., loc. cit.,* (PL 34, 1298-1299).

[48] *Summa Theologica,* II-II, q. 33, a. 5: " . . . si peccator cum
humilitate corripiat delinquentem, non peccat . . . "

[49] *Sententiarum,* lib. 3, c. 32 (PL 83, 704): "Non debet vitia
aliena corripere qui adhuc vitiorum contagionibus servit."

[50] Gregory of Valentia, *Commentaria Theologica, de charitate*
(q. 10, punct. 3). 3, 825.

[51] St. Alphonsus, *Theologia Moralis* (ed. Le Noir). I, 332.

chiel, [52] mentions this twofold obligation. [53] St. Thomas re-marks that:

> as a man ought to give temporal benefits more to those over whom he has temporal care, so also he ought to confer spiritual benefits, such as correc-tion, teaching and the like, more to those over whom he has spiritual care. [54]

Superiors, pastors of souls, parents and teachers, having a greater obligation to care for the spiritual welfare of those under their charge, have a greater obligation than others to correct their delinquent subjects. [55] This follows from the fact that this spiritual care is their special charge and often there is more hope that such correction from them will prove more efficacious. But the common bond of love imposes on all the obligation to help a brother or neighbor in the attainment of the supreme end of man—union with God for all eternity. Thus, one can correct a neighbor who is in the status of spiritual need whether he be superior or equal or inferior to the one in need.

Although a subject is not competent to correct a superior by judicial correction, [56] a subject is still bound by the law of charity to correct a superior who is in spiritual need because of sin. Wycliffe held that a superior should be corrected by the people and that they could remove him from his office. [57] The Council of Constance condemned this teaching, [58] but it does not forbid the correction of a superior by a subject, for, if an inferior corrects his superior, it is not done by way of coercive punishment but in a spirit

---

[52] Ezechiel 33:6.

[53] *De Civitate Dei*, lib. 1, c. 9 (CSEL 40 (1), 17 Hoffman).

[54] *Summa Theologica*, II-II, q. 33, a. 3 ad 1.

[55] Gregory of Valentia, *op. cit., de charitate* (q. 10, punct. 3). 3, 826.

[56] *Cf.*, St. Thomas, *Summa Theologica*, II-II, q. 33, a. 3.

[57] L. Delplace, "Wycliffe and his teaching concerning the Pri-macy," *Dublin Review* 11 (3rd Series, 1884) 23-62.

[58] DBU 597: "Populares possunt ad suum arbitrium dominos delinquentes corrigere."

of love. That an inferior has an obligation to correct a delinquent superior is clear from the very nature of charity.[59] We are bound to correct those who are the objects of our love of charity when they are in need of this correction; and, we are also bound to render help "to him who being in higher position . . . is therefore in greater danger."[60] St. Paul, who was St. Peter's subject, rebuked the chief Apostle, hence:

> Peter gave an example to superiors, that, if at any time they should happen to stray from the straight path, they should not disdain to be corrected by their subjects.[61]

St. Paul, in writing to the Colossians, reminds the people of this obligation for he tells them to "say to Archippus: 'Look to thy ministry, which thou hast received in the Lord, that thou fulfill it.'"[62] Since this act of correction does not require jurisdiction, the subject can correct a superior; for the obligation is founded on love, and this supernatural love of a neighbor ought to be more manifest towards superiors than to others.[63] But when a subject corrects his superior, he must do so with gentleness and respect.[64]

Those who are not superiors are not bound to seek out the sins of their neighbor,[65] but this is an obligation for the superiors. While this added obligation of superiors is clear,

[59] J. de Medicis, *Formalis Explicatio Summae Theologicae S. Thomae Aquinatis* (In II-II, q. 33, a. 2). 6, 693. Cf., Suarez, *Defensio Fidei Catholicae, Et Apostolicae Adversus Anglicanae Sectae Errores* (lib. 6, c. 4, n. 3). 24, 675-676.

[60] St. Thomas, *Summa Theologica*, II-II, q. 33, a. 4 ad 3: " . . . auxilium impartitur ei, qui quanto in loco superiori, tanto in periculo majori versatur."

[61] St. Thomas, *op. cit.*, II-II, q. 33, a. 4 ad 2.

[62] Colossians 4:17.

[63] Gregory of Valentia, *Commentaria Theologica, de charitate* (q. 10, punct. 4). 3,829.

[64] St. Thomas, *Summa Theologica*, II-II, q. 33, a. 4.

[65] St. Thomas, *De Correctione Fraterna*, a. 1 ad 9: " . . . ex praecepto correctionis fraternae non tenemur inquirere peccata aliorum, ut possimus ea corrigere . . . "

Cajetan[66] and Bannez[67] hold that it arises from the obligation of justice, but Valentia,[68] on the other hand, holds that it is an added obligation of charity. With only the personal welfare of his subject in view, he, the superior, would be acting, not as a judge, but as a father. This we call paternal correction.[69] This is not a new precept of charity binding a man after he becomes superior, but rather it is the same precept obliging more strictly and thus the added obligation of investigation into the personal life of a subject.[70]

Fraternal correction has a special importance among the members of the clergy.[71] Being co-workers in the ministry of saving souls, priests, by charitable correction, can give one another mutual aid, not only in obtaining personal sanctification but also in obtaining the salvation of the souls entrusted to their care. Many a grave scandal could be prevented; many an erring brother could be saved; much good accomplished; if fraternal correction were properly and promptly applied by priests to one another.

A point may be raised in connection with the correction of those who are predestined. St. Augustine treated this question and holds that since we cannot distinquish between the predestinate and the reprobate, correction should be given to all who, apparently, stand in need of this spiritual work of mercy.[72]

Although Christ uses the term *brother* in the text of St. Matthew, this does not mean that one is not obliged to correct another who is outside the brotherhood of our faith. Maldonatus would have us understand that our Lord wanted us to correct only Christians.[73] St. Albert the Great understands this obligation to extend to those who are joined with

---

[66] *Comm.* in II-II, q. 33, a. 3.

[67] *De Fide, Spe, et Charitate* (q. 33, a. 3). p. 870.

[68] *Op. cit., de charitate* (q. 10, punct. 3). 3, 825.

[69] *Ibid., de charitate* (q. 10, punct. 3). 3, 827.

[70] *Ibid., loc. cit.*

[71] *Cf.*, L. Ruland, *Morality and the Social Order*, p. 225.

[72] *De Correptione et Gratia*, c. 15, n. 46 (PL 44, 944).

[73] J. Maldonatus, *Commentarii in Quatuor Evangelistas* (In Matt. 18:15). I,364.

us by the bonds of faith, hope, and charity; but, dealing explicitly with the Evangelical Law of correction, he does not exclude, from this act, those to whom we are united merely in the bonds of common brotherhood.[74] It is true that the effects and signs of charity are the result of an inward love,[75] and since the inward act of love is not restricted to those who are of the household of the faith, neither is the charitable act of correction—an external expression of inward love—so restricted. Even though the term *brother* is used and even though this term expressly refers to Christians, those outside the true faith are not excluded from this act of charity. St. Augustine often uses the term *brother* in the exclusive sense of Christian;[76] but he also applies it to the Donatists,[77] although they were sinners and schismatics. He explicitly includes pagans when he deals with the extension of the obligation of fraternal correction, even though they are not *brothers*.[78] It is true that this term was often understood in the restrictive sense of fellow-believers who were united in the bonds of faith; but it also can mean those who are joined in a brotherhood arising from nature and those who are directed to a common destiny.[79] That one is bound to correct another who is not of the faithful can be inferred from the common obligation of prayer. We are bound to pray for all men.[80] But charitable correction, like prayer, is a spiritual work of mercy universal in extent; and it excludes no one from the ambit of this act of love. Both acts confer a spiritual benefit or gift on the recipient. These considera-

[74] *In Evang. Lucae* (17:3). 23, 460.

[75] Cf., St. Thomas, *Summa Theologica*, II-II, q. 25, a. 9, and *In III Sent.* dist. 30, q. 1, a 2.

[76] *De Sermone Domini in Monte*, lib. 1, c. 22, n. 73 (PL 34, 1266): "Fratres autem Christianos significare, multis divinarum scripturarum documentis probari potest."

[77] Cf., *Gesta Cum Emerito*, 3 (CSEL 53, 183 Petschenig).

[78] *De Verbis Domini*, sermo 82, c. 4, n. 7 (PL 38, 509): "Noli illum deputare jam in numero fratrum tuorum. Nec ideo tamen salus ejus negligenda est. Nam et ipsos Ethnicos, id est, Gentiles et Paganos in numero quidem fratrum non deputamus; sed tamen eorum salutem semper inquirimus."

[79] Suarez, *De Charitate* (disp. 8, sect. 2, n. 4). 12, 694.

[80] Cf., St. Thomas, *Summa Theologica*, II-II, q. 83, a. 7.

tions lead to the conclusion that the precept of fraternal correction is universal in nature. All are bound to correct; this act of correction can and should be directed to any person in need of this act of love.

ARTICLE II

THE GRAVITY OF THE OBLIGATION

In treating of fraternal correction, we are dealing with a moral obligation, and not with a mere counsel of perfection. The law of fraternal correction imposes obligations in conscience so that the omission of the required action, given the necessary circumstances, is sinful. Thus, two things have to be established here: that correction imposes an obligation in conscience and that the omission of correction is *per se* a mortal sin.

It is not within the scope of this dissertation to establish the fact that obligations arising from natural law are binding in conscience. Since the natural law is the rule of human actions, any defiance of the law is sinful, for sin is defined as an act contrary to God's law.[81] Whatever is contrary to reason—the proximate rule of morality— is contrary to the eternal law of God, for the natural law is the rational creature's participation in the eternal law of God. The natural law imposes an obligation to correct a delinquent brother. To omit it is sinful, for its omission constitutes an act contrary to God's law.

Sin by definition is "any word, or deed, or desire contrary to the eternal law of God."[82] It is a disordered act, not in agreement with right reason. Thus, St. Augustine would have us understand that all vice is contrary to nature.[83] Going against the prescriptions made known to us by the natural light of reason, constitutes a violation of the rule of reason and, consequently, against the Author

---

[81] St. Augustine, *Contra Faustum*, lib. 22, c. 27 (CSEL 25, 621 Zycha): " . . . peccatum est dictum vel factum vel concupitum contra legem Dei aeternam."

[82] *Ibid., loc. cit.*

[83] *De Libero Arbitrio*, lib. 3, c. 14, n. 38 (PL 32, 1290): "Omne quippe vitium eo ipso quo vitium est, contra naturam est."

of nature.[84]   In this unreasonable act, we will directly not to
follow the order willed by God, as made known to us by
reason, and this is sinful.[85]   It has been shown that the
precept of fraternal correction is of the natural law and
thus it imposes an obligation in conscience; so that its
omission constitutes a violation of the natural order and
therefore such an omission is sinful.   It is also a violation
of Christ's law, but even this can be reduced to an obligation of the natural law, for "the obligation to observe supernatural precepts is always an effect of the natural law."[86]

In the teaching of the Fathers, there is a clear indication
that this obligation of correction is one binding in conscience.
St. Augustine expressly calls the omission of correction a
sin.[87]   When all the required conditions are present, if one
omits this charitable act, the Saint holds that the one omitting the correction is worse off than the sinner himself
and his silence is more reprehensible than the sinner's
action.[88]   St. John Chrysostom shows that the omission of
correction is not only a sin, but a great punishment awaits
those who omit this act of mercy and love.[89]   Basing his
teaching on the obligation of correction, St. Basil shows
that one cannot remain silent when another sins; for, by
our silence, we also sin.[90]   The omission of the prescribed
act of correction is called a sin of taciturnity by St. Gregory
the Great.[91]   St. Bernard brings home this fact of a moral

---

[84] *Ibid.*, lib. 3, c. 14, n. 40 (PL 32, 1291).

[85] St. Thomas, *Summa Theologica*, I-II, q. 71, a. 2 ad 4: "Unde
ejusdem rationis est, quod vitium et peccatum sit contra ordinem
rationis humanae et quod sit contra legem aeternam."

[86] Suarez, *De Legibus*, lib. 2, c. 9, n. 10: " . . . obligatio servandi
supernaturalia praecepta semper est effectus naturalis legis." 5, 120.

[87] *De Civitate Dei*, lib. 1, c. 9 (CSEL 40 (1), 16 Hoffman).

[88] *De Verbis Domini*, sermo 82, c. 4 (PL 38, 508-509).

[89] *Hom. In Epist. ad Hebraeos*, c. 12, hom. 30 (PG 63, 211-212).

[90] *Moralia*, Reg. 52, c. 2 (PG 31, 788). *Cf.*, Origen, *Hom. in Lev.*
hom. 3 (PG 12, 424): "Cum ergo Evangelii tale mandatum sit,
et lex praecipiat, si tacuerit, accipiet peccatum ejus."

[91] *Hom. In Ezech.*, lib. 1, hom. 9, no. 23 (PL 76, 881): "Quae
corrigere non valet, increpare non desinat, ne se participem delin-
quentium ex consensu taciturnitatis addicat."

obligation to correct a delinquent neighbor when he says: "to be silent, when you should correct is to consent: and we know that the same punishment awaits those who do wrong and those who consent to it."[2] Since this obligation arises from an affirmative precept, the omission of correction is a sin of omission."[3]

The omission of fraternal correction is a sin against the virtue of charity. While various rules are given by theologians whereby one can judge the specific nature of an evil act, the Angelic Doctor holds that the essential distinguishing factor in determining the moral species of sin has to be considered in view of the relation of the object to the moral order."[4] Since morality can be predicated only of the actions of an intelligent being, a morally good act consists in the conformity of the particular act to the standard of right reason, while evil consists in the privation of some good demanded by the rule of reason. It is clear that voluntary human actions are specified by their objects,"[5] and hence sins necessarily are distinguished by their objects."[6] The fact that sin is the privation of some good demanded by reason has led theologians to distinguish the sins against God, against self, and against neighbor. This distinction is made because of the moral diversity of the objects of these sins with the threefold order in man; for

> the things whereby man is directed to God, his neighbor and himself are diverse. Thus, this distinction of sins is in respect to their objects, according to which the species of sin are diversified; and consequently this distinction of sin is properly one of different species of sin."[7]

---

[2] *Cf.*, Denis the Carthusian, *Summa De Vitiis et Virtutibus*, lib. 2, a. 41: "Consentire est, tacere quum possis arguere: et scimus quod similes poena facientes maneat et consentientibus." 7, 230.

[3] Merkelbach, *Summa Theologiae Moralis*, I, 353.

[4] St. Thomas, *Summa Theologica*, I-II, q. 72, a. 1. *Cf.*, I-II, q. 71, a. 6.

[5] *Ibid.*, I-II, q. 72, a. 2.

[6] *Ibid.*, I-II, q. 72, a. 1.

[7] *Ibid.*, loc. cit.

Right reason demands that we love our neighbor; and, since the effect of charity should correspond with the affect of charity, external manifestations of this love are demanded by right reason. Now, fraternal correction, being an external manifestation of this love, is also demanded by right reason, so that its omission is contrary to right reason and therefore an evil. This evil, since it violates the order between man and his neighbor, is a *peccatum contra proximum;* but specifically it is contrary to charity.

St. Thomas in his commentary on the *Sentences,* although dealing with the relation of love of enemies to the virtue of charity, establishes principles which may be applied here to show the exact relation of fraternal correction to the same virtue. In those things which pertain to nature and to the possession of grace, a man must love his neighbor, even though he be an enemy.[98] Applying this principle to the question of fraternal correction, since a man must love his neighbor in those things which pertain to nature and to the possession of grace, if he does not manifest·this love, by correction, there is no real love. Man is bound to love all with that love which springs from the virtue of charity.[99] A delinquent sinner, because of his potential relation to God, must be loved with the same love; but this love does not consist only in affective charity, but also in effective charity.[100] The correction of a sinner is a good which we wish for a neighbor and by which we also try to procure, by our well-doing, those things which pertain to his eternal salvation. If one omits this act of correction, there is no love for a neighbor and we fail against both the natural law and against the supernatural law of charity.

There is a twofold relation between man and his neighbor; one arising from the supernatural bond between men and this is the basis of charity; the other, arising from the obligation to give another his due, is the basis of justice.

---

[98] *In* III *Sent.* dist. 30, q. 1, a. 1.

[99] St. Thomas, *De Caritate*, a. 8.

[100] St. Gregory the Great, *Hom. In Evang.*, lib. 2, hom. 30 (PL 76, 1226): "Probatio ergo dilectionis, exhibitio est operis." *Cf.*, St. Thomas, *Summa Theologica*, II-II, q. 32, a. 5.

Both these virtues are necessary in human society, but there is an essential difference:

> Justice looks upon a neighbor as the other one different from self: love sees in him a second self, with whom one desires to be united. Love surrenders its own; justice gives to the other his due.[101]

This difference between justice and charity is clearly expressed by the theologians.[102] It is essential here to point out that the omission of fraternal correction does not constitute a sin against the virtue of justice unless the one bound to correct is the superior of the delinquent. While the subject has a right to the correction of a superior, and while religious and ecclesiastical superiors omitting this act of love would sin both against charity and justice,[103] the omission of simple correction, by a friend who is not a superior, would be violation of charity only. St. Thomas treats of this act of spiritual almsgiving under two aspects; one, personal: inasmuch as sin is harmful to the sinner himself; the other, social: inasmuch as sin is harmful to the common good or harmful to another person. The remedy for the first is a work of charity, and a work of justice is the remedy for the second. As a work of charity, all are obliged to give correction; as a work of justice, correction pertains only to those who have the duty of protecting the common spiritual good—a duty arising from the virtue of justice.[104] Castropalao[105] mentions that some authors hold that one, by the omission of fraternal correction, would also sin against the same virtue violated by the sinner. This opinion is not held by any of the more important theologians, and the authors consulted do not even mention this opinion.

[101] Ruland, *Morality and the Social Order*, p. 14.

[102] Merkelbach, *Summa Theologiae Moralis*, 2, 147.

[103] Gregory of Valentia, *Commentaria Theologica, de charitate* (q. 10, punct. 3). 3, 827.

[104] *Summa Theologica*, II-II, q. 33, a. 1.

[105] *Opus Morale De Virtutibus et Vitiis Contrariis, de charitate* (disp. 3, punct. 1, n. 5). I, 441.

The omission of fraternal correction, when one has the obligation to correct, is a mortal sin *ex genere suo* that is, the gravity of the omission is not absolute *ex toto genere suo mortale* for there can be slight matter in the omission. That the omission of correction is *per se* a grave sin, is clear from the constant and unanimous teaching of the theologians.[106] This teaching flows from the grave obligation one has to aid a neighbor who is in grave or extreme necessity.[107] The grave nature of the obligation is subject to modification in individual cases from the various factors which enter into the consideration of this act of charity.

Basing his opinion on a text taken from St. Augustine,[108] St. Thomas holds that the omission of fraternal correction would constitute a grave sin when one probably could withdraw another from sin, but omits to do so because of some fear or selfish desire.[109] This omission of correction, since it consists in a positive preference of one's own temporal welfare to the spiritual welfare of a neighbor, is manifestly against the proper order of charity.[110].

Per accidens, the omission of fraternal correction may be a venial sin or no sin at all, even though the matter be grave. If one omits correction because, through weakness, one fears to give offense, or feels that the obligation is not grave in the given circumstance, the omission would be a venial sin only, as long as one prefers the sinner's spiritual welfare to his own interests and actually would give correction if it were seen as an absolute condition for the spiritual good of a neighbor. Because of some negligence, which is not gravely culpable, the omission of fraternal cor-

[106] *Cf.,* A. Tanner, *Theologia Scholastica, de spe et charitate* (q. 5, dub. 4, n. 1). 3, 684. Suarez, *De Charitate* (disp. 8, sect. 1, n. 4). 12, 693. St Alphonsus, *Theologia Moralis* (ed. Le Noir). I, 333.

[107] *Cf.,* Merkelbach, *op. cit.,* I, 695.

[108] *De Civitate Dei,* lib. 1, c. 9 (CSEL 40 (1), 17 Hoffman).

[109] *Summa Theologica,* II-II, q. 33, a. 2 ad 3 " . . . hoc [cum peccato mortali] videtur contingere, quando aliquis probabiliter praesumit de aliquo delinquente, quod posset eum a peccato retrahere; et tamen propter timorem vel cupiditatem praetermittit."

[110] *Cf., supra* Chapter I, *fn.* 76.

rection is often a venial sin. The difference in a mortal and venial sin of omission here consists in the fact that the first is directly contrary to charity, while the latter is not. Evidently, this is what St. Thomas has in mind when he distinguishes between the two types of omission for he states that a venial sin is committed:

> when through fear or cupidity, a man is slow to correct his brother's faults, yet not to such a degree, that, if he clearly saw that he could withdraw a neighbor from sin, he would omit it out of fear or cupidity, because in his own mind he prefers charity to these things.[111]

The proper distinction between the omission which is mortal and the omission which is venial seems to rest on the fact that in the venially sinful omission, fraternal love still predominates, so that a man would correct if there were no doubt about its efficacy, while the mortally sinful omission is clearly contrary to fraternal love. Gregory of Valentia, commenting on this passage of St. Thomas, holds that the omission which constitutes a venial sin is not due to love of self but due to some negligence or tepidity without going against the proper order of love.[112] In the first case of grave omission, one acts *contrary* to charity; and in the second case of light omission, one omits fraternal correction *in spite of* fraternal love.[113]

[111] *Summa Theologica*, II-II, q. 33, a. 2 ad 3. *Cf. De Correctione Fraterna*, a. 1 ad 10.

[112] *Op. cit., de charitate* (q. 10, punct. 2). 3, 817.

[113] *Cf.*, Cajetan, *Comm* in II-II, q. 33, a. 2 ad 3: " . . . quando correctio fraterna omittitur vel propter defectum spei . . . vel propter respectum humanum . . . vel quia timet ne illum offendat vel quia timet ne reputetur praesumptuosus; vel ignorantiam . . . si hoc salvatur in praeparatione animi, scilicet quod si crederet probabiliter quod illum a mortale peccato retraheret, omnia postponeret caritati fraternae, non est peccatum mortale . . . Salvatur enim intentio emendationis fratris quam intendit caritas . . . Virtutis autem bonum non tollitur substantialiter salvo bono quod ex fine unde specificatur . . . propter quem defectum veniale peccatum incurritur . . . dum penes dominium vel non dominium passionum in animo supra caritatem fraternam decernitur mortale vel veniale." *Cf.* St. Thomas, *De Correctione Fraterna*, a. 1 ad 10.

Per accidens, the omission of fraternal correction can be even meritorious.

> If anyone forbears to reprove and find fault with those who are doing wrong, because one waits for a suitable time for correcting, or because he fears that, if he does correct, they may become worse, or hinder, oppress or turn away others, who are weak and are in need of being instructed, from the faith, this omission does not seem to result from cupidity, but to be counselled by charity.[114]

This notion will be considered in detail when we deal with the conditions and excusing causes which are attached to the obligation of fraternal correction.[115]

Since the act of fraternal correction entails some inconvenience on the part of the one correcting, it is necessary to consider, briefly, what this obligation entails in the light of the inconvenience or damage to the one exercising this charitable act. Recalling to mind the distinction between extreme and grave spiritual necessity,[116] we can state that if a neighbor is in *extreme* spiritual necessity and it is certain that correction would restore him to grace, one would be bound to correct the delinquent even though there be danger of losing temporal life. The order of charity requires this, for the spiritual necessity of a neighbor—when the necessity is *extreme*—must be placed before all temporal considerations.[117] A case may be envisioned here, where the general rules are applicable. A man dying in mortal sin, who cannot make an act of perfect contrition, does not wish to see a priest. If a friend of this man is certain that his correction will prove beneficial, so that by his plea this dying sinner will see a priest and receive the sacraments, then this sinner must be admonished even

[114] St. Augustine, *De Civitate Dei,* lib. 1, c. 9 (CSEL 40 (1), 16 Hoffman). *Cf.,* St. Thomas, *Summa Theologica,* II-II, q. 33, a. 2 ad 3; *De Correctione Fraterna,* a. 1 ad 10.

[115] *Cf., infra,* p. 67.

[116] *Cf., supra,* p. 14.

[117] *Cf., supra,* p. 14.

though the life of the one correcting would be endangered, as for example by some other member of the family who does not want the dying man to see a priest. In this case, there is certain knowledge of the extreme spiritual need, as well as certain assurance that the correction will prove efficacious. If no one else more bound were willing to carry out this task, then, out of fraternal love, a man would be bound to correct even with the danger of losing his life.[118]

When there is question of a *grave* spiritual necessity, a distinction is necessary. Those who are obliged in virtue of justice to correct a delinquent, even though there is danger of losing life or some other grave detriment, must correct.[119] When there is an obligation of charity only, one would not be obliged to fulfill the obligation when this most grave temporal danger is present.[120] The precept dealing with the relative order between one's temporal goods and the neighbor's spiritual welfare has both a positive and a negative aspect. One may never *positively* prefer a temporal good to a neighbor's spiritual good. Thus, it is never lawful for a man to prefer a temporal good, even life itself, to the spiritual welfare of a neighbor. But when there is question only of a grave spiritual necessity, when one omits correction, the would-be-corrector does not actually prefer his own life or some other temporal good to the spiritual welfare of a neighbor. He knows, however, that the positive aspect of preferring his neighbor's spiritual welfare to his own temporal interests does not oblige in the circumstance.[121] Outside the case of extreme spiritual

---

[118] Billuart, *Summa Sancti Thomae*, 3, 320.

[119] St. Alphonsus, *Theologia Moralis* (ed. Le Noir). I, 332-333.

[120] Billuart, *op. cit.*, 3, 340.

[121] Gregory of Valentia, *Commentaria Theologica, de charitate*, q. 10, punct. 2: Nam cum metu mortis omittitur correptio citra extremam proximi necessitatem, non sit positive contra praeceptum negativum de non praeferenda actu vita propria corporali vitae spirituali proximi [hoc enim non liceret] sed tantummodo se habet quis negative erga vitam corporalem suam et spirtualem proximi, non mandando tunc exsecutioni praeceptum affirmativum de praeferenda vita spirituali proximi vitae propriae corporali, eo quod tunc non obligat cum tanta difficultate."

necessity, charity does not oblige one to aid a neighbor in his spiritual necessity when there is danger of losing life or enduring some other very grave temporal or corporal detriment.[122] However, one is bound to undergo some hardship in the case, but the gravity of this is not a matter for generalization. Each case of hardship or inconvenience has to be judged in the particular circumstance.[123]

One last question about the corrector's obligation. We have already mentioned above that the sinner is bound to correct,[124] but theologians raise the question whether or not a sinner is bound to amend his own ways or repent of his own sin precisely so that he can correct another. The question is: does a sinner commit a new sin if he corrects another without amending his own ways first? When the Fathers hold that the office of correction does not belong to sinners, it is to be understood that they speak of those sinners who do not correct except out of vanity or pride.[125] St. Thomas,[126] Valentia,[127] Tanner [128] and Suarez[129] do not impose the obligation of self correction before one can correct another. St. Thomas considers this question and states:

> the sinner is neither in a state of perplexity nor absolved from the precept of correction: for he is able to abandon his office or also, humbly acknowledging his sin, he can admonish another by entreating him, and then he would not sin.[130]

Self amendment is neither prescribed in the case, nor is it a

---

[122] *Cf.*, Billuart, *op. cit.*, 3, 340.

[123] St. Thomas, *De Correctione Fraterna*, a. 1.

[124] *Cf.*, *supra*, p. 35.

[125] Gregory of Valentia, *op. cit.*, *de charitate* (q. 10, punct. 3). 3, 825.

[126] *Summa Theologica*, II-II, q. 33, a. 5.

[127] *Op. cit.*, *loc. cit.*

[128] *Theologia Scholastica*, *de spe et caritate* (q. 5, dub. 4). 3, 685.

[129] *De Charitate* (disp. 8, sect. 4, n. 6). 12, 699.

[130] *In IV Sent.* dist. 19, a. 2, q. 2 ad 2.

necessary means, for fraternal correction.[131]   *Per accidens,* if the correction by a sinner would cause scandal, then he would have to amend his ways first; but this comes, not from the obligation of fraternal correction, but from the general obligation of avoiding scandal.[132]   It is true that a text of St. Matthew states the Lord's prescription that one must rid self of the *beam* in one's own eye, before attempting to remove the *splint* from the eye of another.[133]   By this text it is understood that a sinner should not correct another sinner in a hypocritical manner so that he may appear just before others.[134]   It can also mean that public sinners should not correct another for secret sins, because of the scandal involved.   Hence, it can be stated that one need not, under the pain of sin, correct himself before administering that correction which arises from the obligation of charity towards a neighbor.

In conclusion to this article, we can clearly see that the obligation of fraternal correction is a moral obligation, binding—*ex genere suo*—under the pain of mortal sin.   At times, the omission of fraternal correction is only a venial sin; while, at other times, the omission can be no sin at all but, on the contrary, it can be an act of virtue.   To be a grave obligation the delinquent must be in mortal sin or in the proximate occasion thereof.   When there is question of extreme spiritual necessity on the part of the delinquent, the precept urges even when there is some grave temporal loss or even fear of death. | In grave spiritual necessity, the obligation is not binding in this manner. but it does oblige when some notable inconvenience or temporal loss can flow from this correction. | A sinner need not mend his ways before he corrects another.

---

[131] Billuart, *Summa Sancti Thomae*, 3, 542.

[132] *Ibid., loc. cit.*

[133] Matthew 7:3-5.

[134] *Cf.,* St. Jerome, *Comm. In Evang. Matthaei,* lib. 1, c. 7 (PL 26, 46-47).   For the meaning of the word hypocrite, *cf., ibid.,* lib. 1, c. 6 (PL 26, 41-42).

ARTICLE III

CONDITIONS AND EXCUSING CAUSES

Since the obligation of fraternal correction arises from an affirmative precept, theologians have set down various conditions and excusing causes which serve as guiding principles in judging a concrete obligation of fraternal correction.[135] The correction of a sinner is an act of virtue, and thus, for its goodness, due circumstances or conditions have to be fulfilled.[136] The authors differ in their listing of these conditions, but an attempt will be made here to enumerate those conditions commonly assigned for the obligation. Although authors are in substantial agreement on these circumstances in general, prudence will always be required in deciding each individual case.[137].

Briefly, the required conditions for a concrete obligation of fraternal correction are:

A. Those required on the part of the one correcting:

1) moral certitude of a neighbor's fault;

2) hope of effecting some good for a neighbor by turning him from sin to the good of virtue;

3) no one else more fit or equally capable to correct, and who will, in fact, admonish the sinner;

4) there must be a proportion between the inconvenience for the one correcting and the good expected on the part of the one corrected.

---

[135] J. Gerson, *De Consolutione Theologiae*, lib. 3, pr. 3: "Correctio fraterna cum sit opus eleemosynae spiritualis, datur sub praecepto affirmativo . . . semper quidem obligat, sed non pro semper." I, 163.

[136] St. Thomas, *De Correctione Fraterna*, a. 1.

[137] *Ibid.*, loc. cit.: " . . . correctio fraterna sub praecepto cadit secundum debitas circumstantias, secundum quod est actus virtutis. Has autem circumstantias determinare sermone, non est possibile, eo quod eorum judicium in singularibus consistit; et pertinet ad prudentiam, vel experimentc et tempore acquisitam, vel magis infusam."

B. Those required on the part of the sinner:

1) the will to be corrected, at least reasonably presumed;

2) little or no probability that, if left to himself, he will return to virtue.

C. Those required on the part of the matter:

necessary matter which certainly includes mortal sin, both material and formal, and most probably venial sin.

Many of these conditions are closely interrelated, and thus they must be considered in detail. The excusing causes flow from the nature of these conditions, for theologians, in general, are agreed that these circumstances must be verified before there is an obligation of giving correction. This is the teaching of Suarez,[138] Valentia,[139] the Carmelite theologians of Salamanca,[140] St. Alphonsus, [141] and Billuart.[142]

Prescinding from the object matter of fraternal correction, which will be treated in the next section, we can see that the first condition required on the part of the one correcting, is knowledge of a neighbor's sin. This is established from the various interpretations given to the text of St. Matthew, for "if thy brother sin *against thee* . . . "[143] The *in te* of the Vulgate has been subject to various interpretations, even though it is omitted in some of the best manuscripts.[144] Some hold that our Blessed Lord is not dealing with fraternal correction in this passage, but rather with the forgiveness of personal injuries. Thus, Palmieri,

---

[138] *De Charitate* (disp. 8, sect. 3). 12, 695-698.

[139] *Commentaria Theologica, de charitate* (q. 10, punct. 2). 3, 808.

[140] *Cursus Theologiae Moralis, de charitate* (q. 7, punct. 4). 5, 154.

[141] *Theologia Moralis* (ed. Le Noir). I, 331-332.

[142] *Summa Sancti Thomae*, 3, 537-540.

[143] Matthew 18:15.

[144] Cf., *Novum Testamentum Graece et Latine* (ed., A. Merk) (*In* Matt. 18:15). p. 60, *fn*.

in a note to Ballerini's treatment of this subject, holds that the passage refers primarily to forgiveness of personal injuries,[145] but, like Maldonatus,[146] he holds that our Lord also gives a precept of fraternal correction. Ballerini, however, understands this text primarily as refering to fraternal correction.[147]

Many texts found in the writings of the Fathers can be advanced in favor of the opinion that this passage is dealing only with personal injuries. Many interpret the *in te* in the sense of *contra te*, as a personal injury. St. Hilary,[148] St. Ambrose,[149] St. John Chrysostom,[150] and St. Jerome,[151] all interpret this text as imposing the obligation of forgiving a personal injury. St. Augustine, however, interprets the *in te*, not only of a personal injury, but also of any offense committed by a neighbor of which one has *knowledge*.[152] This interpretation seems to be the better.

Many theologians understand that *in te* refers to *coram te* or to *te sciente*, and thus understand that this text refers to an obligation to correct when there is moral certitude of a fault on the part of a neighbor. This interpretation can be sustained by passages taken from the Fathers of the Church. St. Basil points out in his *Moralia* that we cannot be indifferent when we *see* another sin, but we must correct him.[153] St. Gregory the Great holds that those who *see* a neighbor sin and remain in silence are guilty of sin.[154] In a

[145] A. Ballerini—D. Palmieri, *Opus Theologicum Morale*, 2, 155 *fn. a.*

[146] *Commentarii In Quatuor Evangelistas* (In Matt. 18:15). I, 365.

[147] *Op. cit.*, 2, 155.

[148] *Commentarius in Matthaeum*, c. 17, n. 7 (PL 9, 1621).

[149] *Expositio Evang. Lucae*, 8, 21 (CSEL 32 (4), 400 Schnekl).

[150] *Commentarius in S. Matthaeum Evangelistam*, hom 50 (PG 58, 583-584).

[151] *Commentarius in Evang. Matthaei*, lib. 3, c. 18 (PL 26,131).

[152] *De Verbis Domini*, sermo 82, c. 7, n. 10 (PL 38, 511): "Peccaverit ergo in te frater tuus, si tu solus nosti, tunc vere in te solum peccavit."

[153] *Moralia*, Reg. 52 (PG 31, 775)

[154] *Regulae Pastoralis Liber*, pars. 3, c. 14 (PL 77, 72): "Qui

letter to Felix of Sicily, the same Gregory points out that one should have knowledge—*veritute cognita*—before proceeding to judicial correction.[155] The same principle, it seems, can be applied to that correction which is fraternal. Origen, although not a Father of the Church, merits mention here. In his *Homily on Leviticus*, he uses the text of St. Matthew and interprets the *in te* in the sense of knowledge of a fault for "if you *see* your brother sin, show him his fault between thee and him alone."[156]

Menoch[157] understands the *in te* in both senses, but Van Steenkiste[158] applies it to a knowledge of another's sin. Tirinus, while holding that our Blessed Lord is refering to a personal injury, holds that this text is also applied to any sin of which we have certain knowledge.[159]

The position of the theologians is quite clear on the meaning of this text, for they are almost unanimous in their interpretation of the text in the sense of fraternal correction, so that one has an obligation to correct a neighbor if knowledge of the neighbor's fault is present. St. Albert the Great understands the *in te in* a twofold sense: as a personal injury and as a sin which is against us inasmuch as the neighbor's sin is an occasion of leading us to sin.[160] If a neighbor's sin is an occasion of our spiritual ruin, then we must certainly have knowledge of the neighbor's act which has at least the appearance of sin. St. Bonaventure insists on this fact of knowledge before proceeding to correction.[161]

enim proximorum mala respiciunt et tamen in silentio linguam premunt, quasi conspectus vulneribus usum medicaminis substrahunt, et eo mortis auctores fiunt, quo virus quod poterant curare noluerunt."

[155] *Epistola ad Felicem in Sicilia*, lib. 9, epist. 44 (PL 77, 976).

[156] *Hom. in Leviticus*, hom. 3, n. 2 (PG 12, 424): "Si videris fratrem tuum peccare argue eum inter te et ipsum solum."

[157] *Comm. Totius Sacrae Scripturae* (*In* Matt. 18:15). 2, 199.

[158] *Sanctum Jesu Christi Evangelium Secundum Matthaeum* (q. 442). I, 698.

[159] *In Universam S. Scripturam Comm.* (*In* Matt. 18:15). 2, 121.

[160] *In Evan. Lucae* (17:3). 23, 460.

[161] *In IV Sent.* (dist. 19, dub. 4). 4, 513. Cf., *Comm in Evan. Lucae*, c. 17: "Dicitur autem peccare in nos quando non solum in personam nostram, sed etiam nobis praesentibus, peccat." 7, 428.

St. Thomas holds that a brother sins against us when his sin is known to us.[162] The interpretation given by the Carmelite theologians of Salamanca is of the same nature.[163] Astesano d'Aste gives this interpretation first and explicitly excludes personal injury from the meaning of the text.[164] Gregory of Valentia[165] and Sylvius[166] also hold this interpretation.

Thus, we can certainly understand the text of St. Matthew[167] to mean that if one has knowledge of a brother's sin, he must correct him if all the necessary conditions are verified. Knowledge is but one of the conditions. Later we will show that the text is not restricted to a personal injury.[168]

One should have knowledge of at least an objective fault on the part of a neighbor. Theologians are in agreement on the quality of the knowledge required, for all, almost without exception, hold that one must have *moral certitude* of another's sin before proceeding to the act of charitable correction. Certitude, in general, is the determination or adherence of the intellect to one thing.[169] Thus, it excludes fear that the opposite is true.[170] The tripartite division of certitude is based on the motives which constitute the formal object. Thus, when we have a firm assent of the intellect

[162] *Quodlibetales,* 11, a. 12.

[163] *Cursus Theologiae Moralis, de charitate,* c. 7, punct. 4, n. 72: " . . . licet illa verba 'si peccaverit in te' plures intelligant de peccato contra singulos commisso . . . intelligitur tamen de omni peccato, quod te sciente committitur." 5, 157.

[164] *Summa Astensis,* lib. 2, tit. 67, a. 4: *"In te* intelligitur, in te scientem, non in te laesum." I, 270.

[165] *Commentaria Theologica, de charitate* (q. 10, punct. 2). 3, 807.

[166] *Comm.* in II-II (q. 33, a. 2, q. 3). 3, 165.

[167] Matthew 18:15.

[168] *Cf., infra.* p. 83-86.

[169] John of St. Thomas, *Cursus Philosophicus Thomisticus, Logica,* pars 2, q. 24, a. 4: "Certitudo . . . nihil aliud est quam determinatio seu adhaesio intellectus ad unum." I, 710.

[170] St. Thomas, *In III Sent.* dist. 26, q. 2, a. 4: "Certitudo autem proprie dicitur firmitas adhaesionis virtutis cognitativae in suum cognoscibile."

arising from the essential necessity of things, we have *meta-physical certitude*.[171] The possibility of error is absolutely incompatible with this type of certitude. When error is impossible according to the laws of nature, we are said to have *physical certitude;* for, judging from objective evidence, a certain fact will always follow except through the miraculous intervention of God.[172] If the motives for giving assent to a proposition are based on objective evidence drawn from the general norms of human conduct, then man is said to have *moral certitude*.[173] That moral certitude which excludes all fear of error and all doubt, is called moral certitude in the strict sense.[174] Moral certitude, in the wide sense of the term, or that certitude which Merkelbach calls "prudential or practical certitude,"[175] excludes all fear of error and also excludes prudent or serious doubt, but it does not exclude the possibility of the opposite being true.[176] If the motives for the assent of the intellect reach such a high degree of probability that a prudent man would be justified in giving his assent without reasonable fear of the opposite, then one is said to have moral certitude.[177] Moralists are agreed that this latter type of moral certitude suffices for prudent action, for the mind here has sufficient motives upon which to base a reasonable judgment.

Moralists also deal with the question of doubt; and it has a practical application, both here, when dealing with the knowledge required of a fault, and later, when we deal with the reasonable hope of success in the obtaining of the objective of this act of love.[178] When the mind wavers between two contradictory propositions, each based on fairly equal motives, a state of *strict doubt* is said to be pres-

[171] Merkelbach, *Summa Theologiae Moralis*, I, 561.

[172] *Ibid., loc. cit.*

[173] *Ibid., loc. cit.*

[174] V. Remer, *Summa Praelectionum Philosophiae Scholasticae*, I, 151.

[175] *Op. cit., loc. cit.*

[176] J. Gredt, *Elementa Philosophiae Aristotelico-Thomisticae*, 2,55.

[177] Merkelbach, *op. cit.*, I, 561.

[178] *Cf., infra*, p. 69-71.

ent.[179]   In a *negative doubt* the reasons why one witholds
assent are so slight that they would never deter a prudent
man from giving his assent; while if there are good reasons
which are solid reasons deterring a prudent man from assent-
ing to either of the propositions, we have a *positive doubt*.[180]
St. Thomas adds, to this classification of the various mental
states, the notion of *suspicion* which he describes as a lack
of firm assent, though the mind is more inclined to one of
the propositions even though this inclination is based on
superficial or slight motives.[181]   Suspicion is the medium
between doubt and opinion, for, as in doubt, there is a lack
of firm assent, but also, as in opinion, there is an inclination
to assent, although this inclination is based on light motives.[182]

Moralists are unanimous in their teaching that *moral
certitude* of a neighbor's fault must be present before there
is an obligation of fraternal love known as fraternal correction.   While a long list of authors could be cited, for
almost all consulted are of the opinion that moral certitude
is required, a few authors will be mentioned in detail because of their extrinsic authority and because of the intrin-
sic value of their arguments.   Navarrus,[183] Suarez,[184] Natalis
Alexander,[185] Castropalao,[186] Gabriel of St. Vincent,[187] the

---

[179] St. Thomas, *In III Sent.* dist. 23, q. 2, a. 2: " . . . homo non
habet rationem ad alteram partem magis quam ad alteram . . . quia
ad utramque habet, sed aequalem, quod dubitatio est." *Cf., Summa
Theologica,* II-II, q. 2, a. 1.

[180] *Cf.,* Remer, *op. cit.,* "Dubium esse potest negativum et
positivum quod adsunt vel non adsunt sufficientes rationes nega-
tionem assensus suadentes." I, 149.

[181] *Summa Theologica,* II-II, q. 2, a. 1. *Cf.,* John of St. Thomas,
op. cit., Logica (pars 2, q 24, a. 4). I, 710.

[182] John of St. Thomas, *loc. cit.:* "Suspicio est assensus in-
clinans in aliquam partem ex aliquo levi signo." I, 710.

[183] *Enchiridion, Sive Manuale* (c. 24, n. 12). I, 140.

[184] *De Charitate* (disp. 8, sect. 3, n. 1). 12, 695.

[185] *Theologia Dogmatica et Moralis* (lib. 4, a. 11). 2, 487.

[186] *Opus Morale De Virtutibus et Vitiis Contrariis, de charitate*
(disp. 3, punct. 4). I, 143.

[187] *De Remediis Ignorantiae* (disp. 2, dub. 6, n. 14). p. 97.

Salmanticenses,[188] St. Alphonsus,[189] and Billuart[190] hold that one must have *moral certitude* of the facts before proceeding to correct a delinquent brother.

While these authors fail to distinguish, in these places, between moral certitude in the strict and wide sense of the term, it is clear that a mere probable opinion of the fact of a neighbor's sin would be insufficient grounds for the concrete grave obligation of correction. Sylvius explicitly excludes the obligation if the knowledge of the sin is only probable.[191] Rocafull,[192] Gregory of St. Vincent,[193] and Billuart[194] assent to this opinion. If, however, the evidence of the neighbor's fault reaches a very high degree of probability, so that it makes the judgment of the fault morally certain, then a man should carry out this act of correction; for in the concrete case he would have that prudential or practical certitude which suffices for a moral action. St. Thomas insists that the obligation of correction has to be carried out along the general lines of prudence.[195] Hence, if—in a particular case—the probability of a neighbor's fault gives moral certitude, in the wide sense of the term, one would be obliged to correct. This is what Gregory of Valentia seems to have in mind when he states that one would not be obliged to correct a neighbor's fault if one does not have *certain* or *probable* knowledge of the fault itself.[196]

---

[188] *Cursus Theologiae Moralis, de charitate* (c. 7, punct. 4, n. 52). 5, 154.

[189] *Theologia Moralis* (ed. Le Noir). I, 333.

[190] *Summa Sancti Thomae*, 3,539.

[191] *Comm. in* II-II, q. 33, a. 2: "Prima conditio est cognitio peccati . . . et quamvis inter omnes non conveniat qualis debeat esse talis cognitio; verius tamen est non sufficere dubitationem, vel quamcumque conjecturalem seu probabilem cognitionem, sed requiri cognitionem moraliter certam." 3, 206.

[192] *Opus Morale in Decalogi Praecepta et Ecclesiae Mandata, tr. de praeceptis 2ae tabulae* (lib. 1, sect. 1, c. 5, n. 107). p. 18.

[193] *Op. cit.* (disp. 2, dub. 6, n. 14). p. 97.

[194] *Op. cit.*, 3, 539.

[195] *De Correctione Fraterna*, a. I.

[196] *Commentaria Theologica, de charitate* (q. 10, punct. 2). 3, 810.

By way of negation, we can hold that one would not be obliged to correct when there is a positive doubt,[197] or conjecture,[198] or suspicion,[199] or a mere probable opinion[200] of the fault which would not be sufficient to move a prudent man to correct in the given case. Since a negative doubt does not destroy moral certitude, if there is but a slight doubt against the conclusion that a neighbor has committed a fault, then one would have to correct for this doubt must be set aside.[201] When dealing with the obligation of corporal almsgiving, a probable or conjectural knowledge of the neighbor's need suffices for action; but the same cannot be said of fraternal correction. The difference consists in the fact that in giving alms of a temporal nature to a person who is only in probable need, there is no danger of giving offense. But if one proceed to correct a neighbor when there is only a probable indication of a need, there certainly would be many an occasion when offense would be given to those corrected; thus it should be omitted.[202]

In their treatment of that moral certitude which is required before one corrects, authors do not state any definite rules or principles dealing with the nature of the objective motives calling for this firm assent of the intellect in a practical case. From the point of view of the manner in which certitude is obtained, theologians and philosophers distinguish between mediate and immediate certitude. If the motive for giving assent to a proposition come from a direct knowledge of the thing, as for example seeing the thing take place, we have immediate certitude. If, however, one gives assent to a proposition because of extrinsic motives, as for example because of the statement of others, we have direct but mediate certitude.

When dealing with the knowledge required of a neigh-

---

[197] Gregory of St. Vincent, *De Remediis Ignorantiae* (disp. 6, dub. 6, n. 14). p. 97.

[198] Sylvius, *Comm. in* II-II (q. 33, a. 2, q. 3). 3, 167.

[199] P. Sporer, *Theologia Moralis super decalogum* (tr. 3, c. 6, sect. 3, n. 91). 1, 473.

[200] Billuart, *Summa Sancti Thomae*, 3, 539.

[201] *Dubium negativum spernendum est.*

[202] Billuart, *op. cit.*, 3, 539.

bor's sin, it might seem that immediate certitude of the fault is required; that is to say, a man would be bound to correct another only when he *sees* a neighbor sin. The interpretation given to the text of St. Matthew, and especially from the interpretation given to the words *in te*,[203] *seems* to be a confirmation of this opinion. One might deduce the necessity of immediate certitude of a neighbor's fault from the teaching of theologians; but this is a *mere* deduction from the use of theological phraseology. Natalis Alexander holds that the precept of fraternal correction is fulfilled sufficiently if one corrects those sinners of whose sin there is an *obvious* knowledge.[204] The Carmelite theologians of Salamanca seem to be of the same opinion.[205] However, one must not exclude that moral certitude of a neighbor's sin which, although known through another, is mediate if, and only if, the testimony is trustworthy. It is true that the interpretations of the text *in te* and the teaching of theologians mentioned seem to require immediate knowledge of the fault; but it can be stated, without hesitation, that, when one only has mediate moral certitude of the fault, one is still bound to correct. The Salmanticenses exclude only that knowledge of a neighbor's sin which comes through hearsay which is a *dubium signum*. But the testimony of another is not always a *dubium signum*, for at times it can give us moral certitude. When Scripture uses the term *in te*, no doubt the meaning primarily refers to those sins of which we have an *obvious* knowledge but it does not exclude this last opinion, that mediate certitude of a neighbor's sin can be a basis for the obligation.

The reason why moral certitude of the neighbor's fault is required is evident. Since the act of fraternal correction

[203] *Cf., supra,* p. 58.

[204] *Theologia Dogmatica et Moralis,* lib. 4, a. 11, reg. 47): " . . . praeceptum correctionis fraternae satis implet, si obvias et coram se peccantes corripiat." 2, 487.

[205] *Cursus Theologiae Moralis, de charitate,* c. 7, punct. 4, n. 52: " . . . talis notitia de exsistentia delictorum in delinquente debet esse moraliter certa . . . unde tantum cognoscens per rumorem, auditum, aut alia dubia signa, proximi peccatum, a correctione abstinere debet." 5, 154.

must be regulated by the rule of prudence,[206] and since it would be most imprudent to correct another for something of which he may be entirely innocent, there is no obligation if this moral certitude is not present. It certainly would be a sin against charity, and not an act of charity, if we would correct those neighbors of whose sin we have only a suspicion or conjecture. We must be morally sure of the neighbor's need before we are bound to give spiritual alms.[207]

When we are in ignorance of the spiritual need of a neighbor, as for example when we have no knowledge of a fault, or when we only suspect a fault, we have no obligation to make inquiries into the conduct of our neighbor.[208] This spying on a neighbor's life would be sinful.[209] Holy Scripture is clear on this point, for we are told to "lie not in wait, nor seek after wickedness in the house of the just, nor spoil his rest."[210] St. Augustine tells us that our Lord warns us not to neglect the sins of a neighbor, but we are not to seek into a neighbor's life in order to find something wrong, but we must correct what we see.[211] We are not bound by the precept of fraternal correction to seek out the sins of a neighbor, even though our intention be directed to the end of correction. It is true that we are bound to seek out the one to whom a material debt is owed, as for example, when we owe money to a creditor; but we are not bound to seek out the spiritual need of a neighbor. The subject has a strict right to the correction of a superior; thus, it is an obligation for the superior to seek out the sins of his subjects.[212] But we cannot apply the same obligation of investigation to fraternal correction. In the case of the superior, the obligation is fixed towards a certain person; but in the matter of fraternal correction the obligation to

---

[206] St. Thomas, *De Correctione Fraterna*, a. 1.

[207] St. Alphonsus, *Theologia Moralis* (ed. Le Noir). I, 332.

[208] Gregory of Valentia, *Commentaria Thologica, de charitate* (q. 10, punct. 2). 3, 810.

[209] Billuart, *Summa Sancti Thomae*, 3, 538.

[210] Proverbs 24: 15.

[211] *De Verbis Domini*, sermo 82, c. 1 (PL 38, 506).

[212] St. Thomas, *Summa Theologica*, II-II, q. 33, a. 2 ad 4.

give a neighbor spiritual aid is not directed to a certain individual but to all sinners in general. Thus, we have to correct only when there is question of evident need. When dealing with culpable ignorance, theologians always insist that one has to be obliged to know some law or fact before culpable ignorance is present. The obligation to know some law or fact comes from a twofold source; *propter se,* because the truth must be known itself—as for example, the fundamental truths of Faith—or *propter aliud,* because of an act which must be placed here and now.[213] There is no obligation to take the means to know the state of a neighbor's soul, for there is no obligation to know the condition of his soul.

It is true, that, by the act of fraternal correction, one shows zeal for the spiritual welfare of a neighbor; but, recalling the words of St. Bernard, one must regulate zeal by knowledge, for:

> *He set in order charity in me.* This is absolutely necessary. For zeal without knowledge is insupportable. Therefore, where zeal is eager, there great discretion—which is the regulation of charity—is necessary. Often indeed, zeal without knowledge is found to be less useful and less effectual: and often it is very dangerous. Thus, the more fervent the zeal, the more eager the spirit, the more profuse the charity, the more need there is for a watchful knowledge which regulates the zeal (of charity), tempers the spirit and orders charity . . . For discretion assigns to every virtue its order.[214]

The second condition is to be judged from the relation of the act of correction to the end proposed. All theologians are agreed that there must be some hope that this act of spiritual almsgiving will prove efficacious in a concrete case. The duty of correcting, then, will depend, in a large measure, on the hope one has of its success. This condition is required, as is evident from the general principles of giv-

---

[213] Billuart, *op. cit.,* 2, 464.
[214] *Sermones in Cantica,* sermo 49, n. 5 (PL 183, 1018).

ing spiritual aid to a neighbor. It is also manifest from the teaching of theologians on the cessation of an obligation, in a concrete case, if the end of the law ceases to exist. Basing ourselves on general principles, with a particular stress on their concrete application, we can perceive that no obligation to correct a neighbor exists if there is no hope of attaining the end of the law, which is the amendment of the sinner.

A general principle, which has a concrete application, may be stated:

> everything that is directed to an end should be proportioned to the end. But acts are proportioned to an end by a certain commensurateness, which results from due circumstances.[215] Among those circumstances which are required for an act of virtue, this circumstance, that an act be proportioned to the end which the virtue intends, seems to be the the principal.[216]

Thus, if a particular act not only fails to attain the end sought by the virtue, but also goes against it, the act, in the concrete, ceases to be virtuous. Now, the end proposed by the law of fraternal correction is the amendment of the sinner. If, in a given case, it is to be hoped that the sinner will be brought back to grace through the instrumentality of our act of correction, this is a virtuous act. However, if the correction will very probably not be effective but will make the sinner worse, then this act is no longer virtuous.[217] In order that the act of correction be proportioned to the end sought, some hope of attaining the end must be present. St. Thomas is explicit on this point for he teaches that:

> fraternal correction is directed to the delinquent's amendment . . . Consequently, when it is deemed

---

[215] St. Thomas, *Summa Theologica*, I-II, q. 7, a. 2.

[216] St. Thomas, *De Correctione Fraterna*, a. 1 ad 1.

[217] *Ibid.*, *loc. cit.*,: "Caritas autem intendit in corrigendo delinquentem, emendationem; unde actus non esset virtuosus, si homo sic corrigeretur, ut inde efficeretur deterior."

probable that the sinner will not receive the admonition, but will become worse, this correction should be omitted, because the means to the end should be regulated by the requirements of the end.[218]

If we have moral certitude that correction will serve as a means to a neighbor's amendment, it is of obligation when all the other circumstances are present. Moral certitude, here, means a reasonable hope of success. If on the other hand, correction will certainly hinder the end proposed, it must be omitted. Between these two types of certitude, one a certitude of the efficacy of correction and the other a certitude of its harmfulness, there are various degrees which have to be considered.

If we have only a *negative doubt* about the hope of success, we should correct; for a negative doubt would not destroy the moral certitude in the case. When dealing with *opinion*, if it is *probable* that the sinner will not accept the correction, or if it is *probable* that the sinner will become worse, then correction should be omitted.[219] Denis the Carthusian,[220] Ledesma,[221] Gerson,[221] Natalis Alexander,[222] and concur in this opinion of the Angelic Doctor. The reason for the omission is clear. Since fraternal correction has the amendment of the sinner for its end, if the correction is likely to prove harmful, even though the harm is only probable, one is obliged to omit it. Conscience, here and now, asserts that the act will probably be harmful, and to

[218] *Summa Theologica*, II-II, q. 33, a. 6.

[219] *Ibid., loc. cit.*

[220] *De Modo Judicandi et Corripiendi*, a. 12: "Correctio ista fraterna, tribus modis omittitur vel differtur. Primo ex caritate et virtuose; ut dum tempus congruum expectatur, vel de peccantis induratione seu deterioratione probabiliter formidatur." 40, 30.

[221] *De Consolatione Theologiae*, lib. 3, pr. 3: "Correctio fraterna . . . omittenda quippe est dum probabiliter apparet quod fieret vel frustra, vel in deteriorationem corrigendi." I, 163.

[222] *Theologia Dogmatica et Moralis* (lib. 4, a. 11, n. 47). 2, 488.

[223] *Theologia Moralis* (tr. 4, c. 4): "Si dubitatur, an frater emendabitur necne, ita ut probabilius sit, quod correctio mea ipsi nocebit, tunc tenear non corrigere." p. 199.

reject this dictate of a practical judgment would be imprudent and sinful.

The question of resolving a *positive doubt*, about the good hoped for and the evil which might result from the correction, is not so easily solved. When the mind wavers between the two contradictory propositions—the possibility of good and the possibility of harm that may result from correction—various principles may aid us in theory, but practical applications entail some difficulty. In the case of doubt of this nature, relative values must be taken into consideration, the greater having precedence over the lesser.[224] This point may be clarified by a few examples taken from the theologians.

If the good expected is superior to the evil feared, then the good takes precedence; and correction must be given. This can be further clarified. If one foresees that the act of correction may cause the sinner to become angry here and now—an evil—but also foresees the probability of an ultimate return to grace, due to this correction, one must administer the correction. The greater good—the ultimate return to grace—is to be preferred to the prevention of anger in the case.[225] Likewise, if a neighbor is dying and is in extreme spiritual necessity and if one is unable to ascertain whether or not the correction will be helpful or harmful to the dying man, one should correct him; for the good of his eternal salvation is to be preferred to the good of freedom from a new sin.[226] Without this correction he would be lost eternally; with it, however, there is a probable hope that it might prove effective, even though there is a probability that, on the contrary, he will commit a new sin. If, on the other hand, the good expected and the evil feared are equal, correction should be omitted, for the negative precept of not injuring a neighbor takes precedence

[224] Billuart, *Summa Theologiae Moralis,*: "Si vero dubium sit an proderit et pariter dubium an nocebit, ut saepe contingit in extraneis et ignotis, cujus ingenium non novimus, conferenda est utilitas sperata cum damno quod timetur, et major est minori praeferendum." 3, 539.

[225] *Ibid.*, 3, 539.

[226] *Ibid., loc. cit.*

over the affirmative precept of procuring a good for him.[227] If one is in doubt about correcting a superior, for example, because of a fear that by this correction, the common good will be injured, correction, again, must be omitted; for the common good—peace of the Church or community—is to be preferred to the good of the individual.[228]

These are general principles, but they can be resolved into the following general classification. If all the other requisites for fraternal correction are present, when there is question of doubt about its efficacy and where the reasons for the hope of beneficial correction and the reasons for the fear of harm to a neighbor are fairly equal and when the doubt cannot be resolved:

1) in the case of extreme spiritual necessity, one should correct;

2) if the good expected and the evil feared are equal, correction should be omitted;

3) if the good expected is much greater than the evil feared, correction should be given;

4) if the evil feared is greater than the good expected, there is no obligation to correct and it even should be omitted.

The obligation of fraternal correction, imposed by the law of fraternal love, ceases, when, in a particular case, there is no hope that it will prove beneficial to the sinner. This, however, has to be understood in the sense that the affirmative *precept* does not cease in this instance, but that the *obligation* does not exist in the given circumstance. Suarez holds that:

the obligation imposed by the affirmative precept of fraternal correction does not cease to exist, when there is no hope of success: but rather, this obligation—which in itself is indefinite—is not in force

---

[227] *Ibid., loc. cit.*
[228] *Ibid., loc. cit.*

for that occasion, since right reason dictates that it is not binding then, inasmuch as the time is not useful nor is the subject properly disposed. As the precept of almsgiving binds one to help those in need; if the aid, however, prove harmful, or if it should be certain that the one in need would not profit by the alms, the precept would not bind, not through a process of cessation nor by epikeia, but because such an occasion would not be one for which the precept— which is a natural precept and not merely of divine law—is binding . . . the reason of the precept can be said to cease, not merely negatively, but also by contrariety: because then correction would not be an act of virtue, but would be idle and useless and it can be harmful, rather than beneficial to one's neighbor.[229]

From another principle of law, it can be shown that in a case of equal doubt about the efficacy of fraternal correction and the harm that might follow from such correction, a man, subjectively, would not sin no matter what he finally chooses to do. For:

if a doubt arises from the concurrence of laws, which cannot be fulfilled at the same time, and a man doubts about what he ought to do, then he can lawfully act against the prescriptions of one law, by fulfilling then and there, after having used moral diligence according to his capacity and the time, whichever he judges in good faith to be the more grave and thus more bound to fulfill, for this man ought not be in a perplexed state, nor does he necessarily sin, for by doing what he can, he satisfies one law and does not transgress the other.[230]

Although there is no conflict between the positive and the negative aspects of love of neighbor, still, in a case of doubt where the doubt cannot be resolved, there seems to be a

---

[229] *De Legibus Ac Legislatore Deo* (lib. 6, c. 9, n. 15). 6, 45.
[230] *Ibid.* (lib. 6, c. 8, n. 12). 6, 38.

conflict of duties, and then that which one judges to be the more grave is of obligation. If he cannot come to a judgment as to which is the more grave, there is no sin, no matter what he chooses to follow. *Objectively*, in a case of equal doubt, one would be bound to omit correction, for the negative precept of not injuring a neighbor is of obligation *semper et pro semper* while the affirmative precept of procuring a good for a neighbor binds *semper sed non pro semper*, depending on various circumstances.

There must be a *necessity* of correction *by us* before we can be obliged to correct another. Since this question of necessity has an intimate relation with the object matter of fraternal correction, this condition will be treated when we deal with those conditions which are required *ex parte materiae*.[231]

The last condition is that a person is not obliged to come to the aid of a neighbor in his spiritual necessity, unless there is a proportion between the inconvenience which one has to undergo and the good expected from this charitable act. Of course, there can be no real proportion between the material and spiritual; but since the obligation is a positive obligation, the inconvenience involved must be considered before there is an obligation of correction. This has already been discussed above,[232] but here we will summarize our conclusions.

1) When a neighbor is in *grave spiritual necessity*, one is not obliged to come to his aid when there is danger of losing temporal life or when there is fear of some other grave temporal detriment. This does not entail a preference of one's temporal good to the spiritual good of a neighbor, but rather the positive aspect of fraternal aid does not apply in the given circumstance. However, one must go to some notable inconvenience to aid the neighbor in this degree of spiritual necessity.

[231] Cf., *infra*, p. 88.
[232] Cf., *supra*. p. 52-54.

2) When a neighbor is in *extreme spiritual neces-sity,* one is bound to correct him, even though there is danger of losing life or there is fear of some other grave evil befalling the person cor-recting. This flows from the very nature of the principles dealing with the proper order of char-ity, for, in the case of extreme spiritual neces-sity, no temporal consideration or benefit can excuse one from not coming to the aid of a neighbor. This holds only if there is certain hope of beneficial correction.

From the above considerations, the *excusing causes* which could be listed here are many; but as these causes which excuse from a concrete obligation of correction are apparent from the treatment of the condition *ex parte corripientis,* they are but listed here.

1) *Lack of certitude* of a neighbor's fault is to be considered as an excusing cause, releasing one from the obligation of correction. Moral certi-tude, at least in the wide sense of the term, is required before there is a concrete obligation of fraternal correction.

2) If correction, outside the cases of extreme spiri-tual necessity, would involve *grave harm* to the one correcting, then there is no obligation to correct.

3) If there is *no hope* of beneficial correction and especially if the correction prove *harmful* to the delinquent, the particular obligation ceases. This is a charitable omission counselled by charity. It is a cessation of the obligation by contra-riety.[233]

4) If there is *no need* of correction *by us,* as in the case where some other person more obliged to

correct is willing to correct, correction can be lawfully omitted. In this case, correction would be of obligation only if the other person failed to carry out his obligation.

Closely allied to the hope which the corrector has of his correction, the first condition *ex parte delinquentis* is that he have the will to accept the correction.[234] If there is no reasonable presumption of this good will, correction should be omitted. Otherwise, the hope of fruitful correction will be in vain. This will to be corrected must be present in the sinner, for without it he is not properly disposed to receive this act of love.[235]

The conditions which are required *ex parte materiae* will be considered in the next section.[236]

ARTICLE IV

THE ORDER OF FRATERNAL CORRECTION

That there is a definite order to be followed in fraternal correction is clear from the words of our Lord, for: "if thy brother sin against thee, go and show him his fault between thee and him alone."[237] This is a clear indication that one should not proceed to a quasi-public or public manifestation of a neighbor's faults until private admonition has proved useless. For:

if he listen to thee, thou hast won thy brother. But if he do not listen to thee take with thee one or two more so that on the word of two or three witnesses every word may be confirmed. And if he refuse to hear them, appeal to the Church, but if he refuse

[234] St. Thomas, *De Correctione Fraterna*, a. 1 ad 2: " . . . duplex est correctio delinquentis; una quidem per simplicem admonitionem; et haec est fraterna correctio, et non habet locum nisi in illis de quibus praesumitur quod propria voluntate admonitioni consentiant . . . "

[235] Suarez, *op. cit.* (lib. 6, c. 9, n. 15). 6, 45

[236] Cf., *infra*, p. 83-104.

[237] Matthew 18:15

to hear even the Church, let him be to thee as the heathen and the publican.[238]

The correct order, then, is that one correct another privately first and, if correction prove inefficacious, then correct before two or three witnesses and finally, if this prove unfruitful, denunciation to the Church or to the legitimate superior of the sinner.

We shall first examine the interpretation of this text as given by the Fathers; and then prove that the stated order of fraternal correction—private admonition before a public manifestation of a neighbor's fault—is a matter of precept. Finally, we shall indicate those circumstances in which, for a particular reason, one may proceed to a public manifestation immediately.

Commenting on these words of our Lord, St. Augustine teaches that private admonition should be given in the first place, for our aim and intention is to lead a brother from the evil of his ways. If we correct him before others, he might defend himself; and thus, instead of making him better, we would make him worse.[239] St. Ambrose shows that this manner of private admonition is in conformity with right reason.[240] St. Hilary[241] and St. John Chrysostom[242] indicate that private mode of correction should precede any public denunciation. This matter was also treated by Origen, for he states that our Blessed Lord does not want us to manifest a neighbor's sin publicly, but rather, when we see him sin, our correction should be private.[243]

With the notable exception of St. Bonaventure, who holds that the order mentioned in the Gospel is not obligatory

[238] *Ibid.*, 18:15-17.
[239] *De Verbis Domini*, sermo 32, c. 4 (PL 38, 509).
[240] *Expositio in Psalmum* 118, 8, 32 (CSEL 62, 169).
[241] *Commentarius in Matthaeum*, c. 18, n. 7 (PL 9, 1021).
[242] *Hom. in Matt.*, hom. 60 (PG 58, 536).
[243] *Hom. in Leviticus*, hom. 3, n. 2 (PG 12, 424).

but merely fitting,[244] theologians, in general, hold that the order is a matter of precept. The reason for the prescribed order is that we may safeguard the good name of the sinner —to which we are bound by charity.[245] The end of correction is the amendment of the sinner, but if we correct him publicly, before having attempted private admonition, we endanger his right to a good name and he may become hardened in his sin.[246] The prescribed order is not only of positive divine law but it is also a precept of natural law, for the natural law requires that we do for others what we wish done for ourselves. If we stand in need of correction, it is only reasonable that we wish it done in the least harmful way, that is, privately. St. Thomas points out the reasonableness of this order, for if a man has already lost his good name by a public manifestation of his sins, he will consider future sins as a light matter.[247] St. Jerome attests to this fact, that private admonition should be given first, for if a neighbor has lost his good name, often he will remain in sin.[248] To manifest publicly the sins of our neighbor, when there is no reason for doing so, will often be a cause of scandal to others. Hence, private admonition should be the first mode of procedure.

[244] *In Evang. Lucae*, c. 17: "Hic autem ordo congruitatis est, non necessitatis, et maxime, si percipiatur, quod proximus incorrigibilis est ad verbum fratris, sed tantum in manu forti . . . " 7, 428.

[245] St. Thomas, *De Correctione Fraterna*, a. 2: "Haec est igitur ratio hujusmodi ordinis servandi in correctione fraterna, ut parcatur pudori fratris, ne deterior efficiatur. Sed ad hoc tenemur per praceptum caritatis. Ergo ordo correctionis fraternae cadit sub praecepto."

[246] St. Thomas, *Summa Theologica*, II-II, q. 33, a. 7.

[247] *De Correctione Fraterna*, a. 2: " . . . bona fama est praecipuum inter bona exteriora . . . Sicut igitur peccaret qui absque necessitate ingereret alicui divitiarum dispendium; ita, et multo amplius, peccat si aliquis absque necessitate proximo ingereret dispendium famae, absque necessitate ejus peccatum publicando . . . propter conservationem famae homo multoties abstinet a peccatis. Et ideo, quando aliquis videt se jam famam amisisse, pro nihilo ducit peccare."

[248] *Comm. In Evang. S. Matthaei*, lib. 3, c. 18 (PL 26, 131): "Corripiendus est autem frater seorsum, ne si semel pudorem aut verecundiam amiserit, remaneat in peccato."

When there is a reasonable hope that correction will prove efficacious, if the sin is *occult,* the secret mode of correction must be followed.[249] This correction *between thee and him alone* should be followed and even repeated as long as there remains this reasonable hope of converting the sinner from his evil ways.[250] If there is no hope of aiding him by the secret mode, we must proceed to correction before two or more witnesses, when there is hope that this will prove beneficial to the sinner.[251] This is the middle course between secret correction and public manifestation before a superior.[262] This manifestation of another's sin before trustworthy people is not sinful, for it does not dishonor the sinner before the public.[253] If there is no hope that this middle mode of correction will prove efficacious, then, ordinarily, it must be omitted.[254] For where the end of fraternal correction becomes impossible, the means to the end are not of obligation. If both the private and middle mode of correction prove ineffectual, then we must inform the delinquent's superior of the fault if there is hope that the sinner can be converted to virtue by his superior.

St. Augustine holds that, before one brings in two or more witnesses, the fault of the neighbor should be made manifest to the superior.[255] This is to be understood in the sense that, before bringing in witnesses, appeal should be made to the superior, as a father or as a private individual but not as a judge; for in the matter of fraternal correction, he is often able to do more by acting through paternal correction than another can do by manifesting the sin of a

[249] St. Thomas, *Summa Theologica,* II-II, q. 33, a. 7.

[250] *De Correctione Fraterna,* a. 2 ad 23: " . . . cum Dominus dicit, *Corripe inter te et ipsum solum,* non intelligendum est quod semel corripiatur, sed bis vel ter, aut etiam pluries, quamdiu probabiliter spes maneat quod secretius corripi potest."

[251] *Ibid.,* a. 2 ad 2.

[252] St. Thomas, *Summa Theologica,* II-II, q. 33, a. 8.

[253] *Ibid., loc. cit.*

[254] St. Thomas, *De Correctione Fraterna,* a. 2, ad 2.

[255] *Regula ad Servos Dei,* n. 7 (PL 32, 1381): "Sed antequam aliis demonstretur, per quos convincendus est, si negaverit, prius praeposito debet ostendi . . . " Cf., Hugh of St. Victor, *Expositio in Regulam Beati Augustini,* c. 7 (PL 176, 902).

neighbor before two or three witnesses.[256] This would not be contrary to charity, nor contrary to the proper order of correction, for, here, the superior is not acting as a judge but as a father.

Even though a neighbor's sin be occult, there are times when public denunciation can precede a private admonition. When there is danger to the common good or when there is danger of an evil befalling another person due to another's sin, private admonition can be omitted and recourse can be made directly to the superior.[257] In this case, the spiritual or temporal welfare of the community must be considered before the good name of the delinquent[258] Even if there is no general danger to the community, if the sinner by his occult sin is leading others to sin, denunciation must be made immediately to the superior; for there is a greater obligation of protecting others from spiritual or corporal harm, than there is to protect the good name of a delinquent.[259] This type of sin, although occult, is to be considered as a public sin *per accidens, i. e., in se* occult, but, due to attending circumstances of scandal or grave harm, equivalent to a public sin. If, however, the evil can be prevented *with certainty* by a secret admonition, then one must admonish in private;[260] for the circumstances calling for public denunciation cease to exist.

---

[256] St. Thomas, *op. cit.,* a. ad 26: " . . . Augustinus intelligit quod prius dictatur praelato quam testibus, secundum quod praelatus est quaedam singularis persona, quae potest prodesse etiam magis quam alii. Sic autem dicere praelato, non est dicere Ecclesiae; sed quando dicitur in publico, quasi in loco judicii residenti."

[257] St. Thomas, *Summa Theologica,* II-II, q. 33, a. 7.

[258] St. Thomas, *De Correctione Fraterna,* a. 2 ad 7: " . . . non in omni peccato debet homo procedere ad accusationem; sed solum in illis peccatis ex quibus in promptu est ut proveniat periculum multitudini, vel spirituale vel corporale. Tunc enim potest homo ad accusationem procedere, monitione non praecedente, si hoc exigat utilitas communis; quia bonum commune praeferendum est bono privato."

[259] Billuart, *Summa Sancti Thomae,* 3, 542.

[260] St. Thomas, *Summa Theologica,* II-II, q. 33, a. 7: "Quaedam enim peccata occulta sunt quae sunt in nocumentum proximorum, vel corporale, vel spirituale . . . oportet statim procedere ad denuntiationem ut hujusmodi nocumentum impediatur; nisi forte

When dealing with sins which are public *per se* or *per accidens,* and when the common good is at stake, the direct manifestation to the superior is to be made immediately, even though there is no hope of correcting the sinner.[261] The reason is clear; for this denunciation intends, primarily, to impede injury to a community or to an innocent person. This obligation of denunciation can be placed on a person by a confessor under the pain of denial of absolution.[262]

The prescribed order of fraternal correction is equally applicable to religious. St. Thomas points out that, if a superior would command a subject to reveal the faults of another when there is hope that private correction will suffice, the superior is not to be obeyed.[263] Thus, in keeping with general principles, if a superior would expressly command something contrary to the order established by our Lord, both the superior and the one obeying would sin. In some religious rules, there *seems* to be a violation of the order established by our Lord; but these prescriptions are to be interpreted in conformity with the order mentioned by Christ. Thus, whenever a command of a superior seems to be against the order of fraternal correction, the command is to be understood with the proviso "saving the order of fraternal correction."[264] In the rule of the Society of Jesus, we find the following prescription:

For the greater progress in spirit, and especially for higher submission and self humility, everyone

---

aliquis firmiter aestimaret, quod statim per secretam admonitionem posset hujusmodi mala impedire."

[261] Billuart, *op. cit.,* 3, 539

[262] Merkelbach, *Summa Theologiae Moralis,* I, 720

[263] *Summa Theologica,* II-II, q. 33, a. 7 ad 5. Cf., *Quodlibetales,* 11, a. 13.

[264] St. Thomas, *Summa Theologica,* II-II, q. 33, a. 7 ad 5: ". . . si praelatus expresse praeciperet contra hanc ordinem a Domino institutum, et ipse peccaret praecipiens, et ei obediens, quasi contra praeceptum Domini agens . . . quando praelatus praecipit ut sibi dicatur quod quis sciverit corrigendum, intelligendum est praeceptum sane, salvo ordine fraternae correctionis; sive praeceptum fiat communiter ad omnes, sive ad aliquem specialiter."

should be content that all his errors and defects, and all things whatsoever have been noted in him, should be made known to the superiors by anyone who has knowledge of them outside of confession.[265]

Commenting on this prescription of the rule of his order, Suarez clearly states that all defects, even grievous sins which are occult, should be manifested to the superior—even without previous private admonition.[266] He shows that it is not contrary to the order established in the Gospel, for there is no place in the Gospel which confers on anyone the right to be admonished by a brother before being admonished by a father, if one wishes to be corrected in the more perfect way. He rightly concludes that this denunciation to a superior as a father, without previous private correction, is not contrary to charity nor is it contrary to the natural and Evangelical precept dealing with the proper order of fraternal correction.[267] St. Thomas also holds that if one sees that correction by a superior, acting not as a superior but as a father, will prove more efficacious than a private admonition, one could lawfully make the fault known to the superior without having first admonished the delinquent privately.[268]

In general then, the external order of fraternal correction is that mentioned in our study. When possible, admonition should first be given privately, and then, if necessary, the medium way of calling in witnesses should be employed before accusation is made to a superior.

Fraternal correction must be carried out in a kindly manner, for we should avoid anything that would irritate or discourage the sinner.[269] Since it is out of love that we correct a brother, we should use the means best fitted to

---

[265] Suarez, *De Religione* (lib, 10, c. 7, n. 2). 16, 1090.

[266] *Ibid., loc. cit.*

[267] *Ibid.* (lib. 10, c. 7, n. 20). 16, 1097. *Cf., De Charitate* (disp. 8, sect. 6, n. 11). 12, 704.

[268] *Quodlibetales*, 11, a. 13.

[269] N. Alexander, *Theologia Dogmatica et Moralis* (lib. 4, reg. 56). 2, 491.

bring about this effect.[270]   If we are harsh in our correction of others, often we shall turn the sinner against us and perhaps destroy all hope of amendment. St. John Chrysostom points out that a doctor is often successful with a patient because of his kindness. In like manner, if we wish to correct a brother, we should show our charity towards him and try to persuade him by our correction and advice that we do not wish to put him to shame but rather to guide him and cure him of this malady of sin.[271]

A rebuke, carried out in the spirit of love, must be kind. For this kindness will make a sinner feel ashamed of his sin, while harshness will only provoke him to indignation.[272] It is much better that the sinner look upon the one correcting him as a true friend, for the sinner's heart will be moved to repentance more readily by a kind and gentle counsel than by harsh words.[273] St. Bernard distinguishes between two types of correction; one of kindness, which should be the general rule, and the other severe rebuke, which is reserved for those on whom a mild admonition will prove inefficacious.[274] However, in fraternal correction, we should follow out the obligation of rebuke in the most kind manner. In this way, it will be easy to win the heart and confidence of the sinner, while sarcasm and ridicule will only turn the sinner away.

---

[270] St. Augustine, *De Verbis Domini*, sermo 82, c. 3, n. 4 (PL 38, 507): " . . . debemus amando corripere . . . non nocendi aviditate, sed studio corrigendi . . . Quare illum corripias? Quia te doles, quod peccavit in te? Absit. Si amore tui id facis, nihil facis. Si amore illius facis, optime facis."

[271] *De Statuis*, hom. 3 (PG 49, 54).

[272] St. Ambrose, *Expositio Evang.* Lucae, 8, 21 (CSEL 32 (4), 400 Schnekl).

[273] *Ibid., loc. cit.*

[274] *Sermones in Cantica*, sermo 44 (PL 183, 996).

B—OBJECT

Introduction:

It is quite generally agreed that sin is the object or subject matter of fraternal correction. This question, dealing with the object of correction, is in reality two distinct, yet mutually related, questions. This first, relating to the nature of the sin many be stated thus: what class of sins fall under the prescriptions of fraternal correction? That is, is the object of this act restricted to personal offenses committed against us, or may it be extended to all sin? The second question relates to the adequate object of this act of love. Is correction restricted to mortal sins alone, or may it be extended to include venial as well as material sin? Of these two questions, more attention will be directed to the second; but the first is also of importance. Here, we are not dealing with the objective or aim of fraternal correction, but rather with the material object of this act of fraternal love.

It would not be difficult to list several passages from the Fathers of the Church which would seem to indicate that the precept of fraternal correction, as stated in St. Matthew's Gospel, deals with the obligation incumbent upon man to forgive a neighbor for personal offenses committed against him. In fact, the context seems to bring this interpretation out, for the whole theme seems to treat of brotherly love and the forgiveness of injuries. While some of the Fathers do not exclude from the interpretation of this text the notion of fraternal correction, as applying to all sin, others clearly point out that our Lord is here dealing only with the forgiveness of personal injuries.

St. Hilary applies the text to forgiveness of personal injuries,[1] while St. Ambrose, treating of the text in connection with a parallel text of St. Luke, certainly understands it in a restrictive sense, showing that sins against God and against man are not the same.[2] St. Jerome explicitly ex-

---

[1] *Commentarius in Matthaeum*, In Matt. 18, n. 7 (PL 9, 1021).
[2] *Expositio Evang. Lucae*, In Lk. 17, 3 (CSEL 32 (4), 401 Schnekl).

cludes sins against God from the scope of this text and restricts the interpretation to a personal injury for:

> if our brother sin against us and injure us in any
> way, we have the power, and indeed the obligation,
> to forgive him, for it is prescribed that we forgive
> our debitors their debts. If, however, anyone sin
> against God, this is not within our power.[3]

St. Basil uses this text of St. Matthew to show that we
must be patient with a neighbor who injures us and we must
offer prayers for those who have thus offended us.[4] These
are but a few of the Fathers who understand this text in a
restrictive sense.

If the *in te* of the Vulgate, which is omitted in some of
the manuscripts, were omitted here, then we would have a
clear indication of the precept of fraternal correction extend-
ing to all sin. The text then would read: "If thy brother
sin, go and show him his fault . . . " This would not limit
th meaning of the text to the restrictive sense of a "sin
against thee." However, even if we consider the *in te* as
part of the text, we believe it can be shown that it does not
limit our obligation to the correction or forgivness of personal injuries. In fact, some of the Fathers, while giving the
restrictive meaning, also include the notion of fraternal correction for all sin.

When St. Augustine treats of this text, he takes the *in
te* in the sense of knowledge of another's sin.[5] He also
warns us that we are not to search into a neighbor's life in
order to find something which needs correction, but we are
bond to correct only those things which we see.[6] If this
precept were not to be understood of all sin, why would St.
Augustine have to warn us not to go looking for evil? For
if it were to be understood of a personal injury only, certain-

---

[3] *Commentaria in Evang. Matthaei*, lib. 3, c. 18 (PL 26, 131).

[4] *Regulae Brevius Tractatae*, int. 232 (PG 31, 1238).

[5] *De Verbis Domini*, sermo 82, c. 7, n. 10 (PL 38, 511: "Peccavit
ergo in te frater tuus, si tu solus nosti, tunc vere in te solum
peccavit."

[6] *Ibid.*, sermo 82, c. 1 (PL 38, 506).

ly we would know about it without seeking into the life of another. Evidently, he is dealing with the correction of all sins which are evident to us, whether or not these sins are against us, against God, or against our neighbor. Elsewhere, St. Augustine gives us a good example of correction when the sin is not against us, that is, when the sin is not a personal injury, for:

> if you see your brother hurrying off to the theatre, dissuade him, admonish him and show him your concern . . . If you see others going off to get drunk and they wish to enter into a sacred place in such a condition . . . hinder them if you can.[7]

St. John Chrysostom also gives an example of correction, when the delinquent does not injure us personally. He teaches that:

> If you see a friend going into fornication, say to him: 'Thou art going after an evil thing, are you not ashamed, do you not blush? This is wrong.' Do you reply that he knows that this is an evil? Certainly he knows it, but he is drawn by passion. A sick man also knows that cold water is bad for him, yet he needs some one to prevent him from taking it . . . if you see your friend going off to get drunk or going to a banquet where there is much drunkeness, then do the same (correct and admonish) for him . . . This is friendship: brother aided by a brother becomes a fortified city. (Prov. 18:19) . . . if we are friends, if we truly care for one another, let us help one another in this regard: this leads to a profitable friendship; let us hinder those things which lead to hell.[8]

St. Thomas answers the objection which might be raised from the teaching of St. Jerome,[9] when he says that it is not

---

[7] *Tractatus in Joannis Evangelium,* tr. 10, c. 2, n. 9 (PL 35, 1472).

[8] *Enarratio in Epistolam ad Hebraeos,* c. 12, hom. 30 (PG 63, 212).

[9] *Cf., supra,* p. 84.

our business to forgive sins committed against God, for although this statement of St. Jerome is true, it certainly is our business to correct our neighbor and to follow out the order established by Christ.[10]   The teaching of theologians on this point is clear.   All are agreed that it makes no difference, as far as the obligation of fraternal correction is concerned, whether or not the sin is directly against God, against ourselves, or against our neighbors.[11] This is a reasonable position, for we are dealing with the care of the spiritual life of a neighbor which can be in danger from any grave sin.   The obligation is not restricted to personal injury, for the precept deals, not with the removal of personal injury, but with the saving or winning of a brother's soul, which is connected with any mortal sin.

We have already explained the meaning of *in te* in the sense of any sin of which we have knowledge.[12]   It was then pointed out that some of the theologians consider the phrase to have the meaning of any sin which can be a cause of scandal to us.   Any sin—against God, self or neighbor—can be a cause of scandal; so it can be stated with certitude that all sins fall under the subject matter of fraternal correction.

ARTICLE I

MORTAL SIN AND FRATERNAL CORRECTION

We have just seen that the obligation of charitable correction is not restricted to personal injuries.   In this article we will discuss formal mortal sin; the question of fraternal

---

[10] *De Correctione Fraterna*, a. 2 ad 20.

[11] Toletus, *In Summam Theologiae S. Thomae Aquinatis Enarratio*, In II-II, q. 33, a. 2: "Non solum corrigenda peccata quae contra nos fiunt, sed etiam quae coram nobis proximum committuntur, aut contra Deum, nam per omnia salus ipsius peccantis perditur, quam qui potest, curare debet." 2, 208: *Cf.*, Sylvius, *Comm.* (II-II, a. 33, a. 2).   3, 163:   Astesano d'Aste, *Summa Astensis* (lib. 2, a. 4).   I, 270:   J. de Medicis, *Formalis Explicatio Theologiae S. Thomae Aquinatis* (II-II, q. 33, a. 7).   6, 403:   N. Alexander, *Theologia Dogmatica et Moralis* (lib. 4, reg. 39). 2, 485.

[12] *Cf.*, *supra*, p. 58.

correction relative to venial and material sin will be treated in the next article.

Mortal sin, which deprives the soul of the divine life of grace, is the proper matter for the object of this act of love. This is clear from the text under consideration for, after correction, "if he listen to thee thou hast won thy brother."[13] The purpose of fraternal correction is to give spiritual aid to one who is in danger of losing his soul. Certainly, this danger is present after mortal sin; for if one dies in this state, salvation is absolutely impossible. The obligation to correct depends on the neighbor's spiritual need. We have defined this need as grave, when a man finds great difficulty in returning to grace without some outside help.[14] If left to himself, the sinner will find great difficulty in avoiding eternal damnation. This consideration of grave spiritual necessity arises from a twofold consideration; objectively, the presence of mortal sin, and subjectively, the great difficulty which a man has, in a concrete case, to obtain forgiveness of his sin without some help from a neighbor. Thus, objectively speaking, or as a condition required *ex parte materiae*, any mortal sin is sufficient matter for fraternal correction.

St. Augustine, in discussing the words "thou hast won thy brother," interprets them as meaning that we are saving a brother from eternal perdition.[15] Consistently, he refers to the fact of a brother being in danger of perishing if we omit correction. If, by our silence, we let a brother perish, we are no longer holy or innocent.[16] Since it is impossible to know those who are among the predestined, we must correct all who stand in apparent need of correction, so that they will not perish.[17] St. John Chrysostom speaks in the same manner, for he holds that, in the matter of correction, we are dealing with the everlasting life of our neigh-

---

[13] Matthew 18:15.
[14] *Cf., supra*, p. 14.
[15] *De Verbis Domini*, sermo 82, c. 4 (PL 38, 508-509).
[16] *Regula ad Servos Dei*, 7 (PL 32, 1381).
[17] *De Correptione et Gratia*, c. 15, n. 46 (PL 44; 944).

bor's soul; if we fail to aid him, when we are able to do so, the penalty will be great.[18]

The teaching of the theologians is unanimous on this point. All agree that the proper object of fraternal correction is mortal sin. This teaching of the theologians is based on the text of St. Matthew and upon the general principles obliging one to come to a neighbor's aid, when he is in grave or extreme spiritual necessity. For example, the Carmelite theologians of Salamanca hold that mortal sin is the matter for fraternal correction and their reason is adduced from the interpretation of "thou hast won thy brother."[19] Denis the Carthusian shows that this text means that we have snatched the sinner from the burden of sin and from eternal damnation.[20]

From the general principles of one's obligation to aid a neighbor in grave or extreme spiritual necessity, we know that he has to be in actual need before this aid is of obligation.[21] This, as has been indicated, entails a twofold consideration of the need—objective and subjective—but here we will first consider the objective elements constituting this need. When the theologians deal with this matter, there is considerable controversy, but we will point out the established teaching before considering those points which bring us into the realm of controversy.

Since the end of fraternal correction is to withdraw a neighbor from sin, fraternal correction is not of obligation if our neighbor has already returned to virtue.[22] We cannot have absolute certitude of this fact of the return to grace or of his will to do better,[23] but if the sinner promises to

[18] *Enarratio in Epistolam ad Hebraeos*, c. 12, hom. 30 (PG 63, 212).

[19] *Cursus Theologiae Moralis, de charitate* (c. 7, punct. 4 n. 45). 5, 154.

[20] *Enarratio in Evang. Secundum Matthaeum*, (In Matt. 18, a. 32). 11, 207.

[21] Cf., *supra*, p. 15.

[22] Suarez, *De Charitate* (disp. 8, sect. 3, n. 7). 12, 697.

[23] St. Augustine, *De Civitate Dei*, lib. 1, c. 9 (CSEL 40 (1), 17 Hoffman): " . . . semper incertum est utrum voluntatem sit in melius mutaturi"

amend his ways, this would seem sufficient for, as St. Thomas holds, it would be a sin for us to manifest the neighbor's sin, even to a superior, if he has given this promise to amend his life.[24] The necessity is no longer present, and since the means of fulfilling an obligation should be regulated to the requirements of the end,[25] if the end has been attained otherwise, the means to the end are not of obligation.

The second point of general agreement among theologians deals with those sinners who have committed a grave sin and have not amended their ways and now are in danger of relapse into grave sin. All hold that one is obliged to help this neighbor, for objectively, we have the necessary matter—mortal sin still on a neighbor's soul— and, subjectively, the man is unable to help himself as is evidenced by the fact that he is in the danger of falling back into the same sin or another sin of equal gravity. Here, we have a practical certitude that a neighbor is in need of correction, for without it there will be a relapse into sin. The obligation to correct rests on the fact that there is a need, for we have no reasonable hope that he will come to his own aid and no hope that another will aid him.[26]

It is not easy to determine the obligation of fraternal correction relative to the *status peccati*. The *status peccati* is defined as a state of habitual aversion from God which will last until the soul is freed from mortal sin by penance.[27] Here, we deal with a mortal sin committed by a neighbor, who has not as yet repented, and is not now in the proximate danger of relapse into sin and is not in danger of death. Theologians differ as to the obligation of fraternal correction in this case. Gregory of St. Vincent,[28] De Co-

[24] *De Correctione Fraterna*, a. 2 ad 19: " . . . ille qui peccavit emendationem promittit, contra praeceptum Dei ageret qui socium peccantem vel ad praelatum vel ad alium deferret."

[25] St. Thomas, *Summa Theologica*, II-II, q. 33, a. 6.

[26] Suarez, *De Charitate* (disp. 8, sect. 3, n. 7) 12, 697.

[27] A. Tanquerey, *Synopsis Theologiae Moralis et Pastoralis*, 2, 354.

[28] *De Remediis Ignorantiae* (disp. 2. dub. 6, n. 14). p. 96.

ninck,[29] and Catalanus,[30] may be mentioned among those who hold that one is not obliged to correct this sinner, as long as there is no danger of relapse into sin. The more probable opinion, however, is that there is an obligation of charitable correction in the stated case. This is the teaching of Bannez,[31] Ledesma,[32] the Salmanticenses,[33] and St. Alphonsus.[34]

Those who deny the obligation of fraternal correction in the stated case place all the weight of their arguments on the fact that a sinner does not have the obligation to return to the state of grace immediately after a fall into mortal sin. Thus, if one were bound to correct a sinner when there is no danger of a relapse into sin, the one correcting would be more bound to take care of the spiritual welfare of a neighbor than would the neighbor himself.[35] The basis of the affirmative opinion rests on the fact that the sinner, in a state of sin, is in grave spiritual necessity—objectively—; and subjectively, the sinner has to be corrected by another for there is a fear that if it is omitted, the sinner will probably fall into other sins or will remain in the same sin for a long time.[36] If, however, a man knows that the sinner will soon return to grace without his aid, there is no need of correction.[37] If the correction is necessary for his return to grace, given the opportune time and given the case of grave spiritual necessity, a man must correct the delinquent, even though there is no danger of a relapse into sin, for:

if there is a necessity, given the opportune time

[29] *De Moralitate* (lib. 4, disp 28, dub. 4). p. 573.

[30] *Universi Juris Theologico-Moralis Corpus Integrum* (pars. 1, q. 7, c. 6). I, 168.

[31] *De Fide, Spe, et Charitate* (q. 33, a. 2). p. 870.

[32] *Theologia Moralis* (tr. 4, c. 4). p. 194.

[33] *Cursus Theologiae Moralis, de charitate* (c. 7. punct. 4, n. 50). 5, 154.

[34] *Theologia Moralis* (ed. Le Noir). I, 332.

[35] Gregory of St. Vincent, *op. cit.* (disp. 2, dub. 6, n. 14). p. 96.

[36] Suarez, *De Charitate* (disp. 8, sect, 3, n. 7). 12, 697.

[37] *Ibid., loc. cit.*

with the other circumstances, this precept of fraternal correction obliges immediately . . . For given the time of necessity, nothing else can be reasonably expected, especially since it is hard to find an opportune time for beneficial correction, and when this time occurs with probability and the necessity is present, it is not lawful to neglect correction. From which fact, a man is sometimes bound to correct his neighbor immediately, even though the sinner himself is not bound to repent immediately; for the sinner is master of his own will and can always find an opportune time for repentance; and if he does not repent here and now, he may perhaps be excused because he does not advert to the danger in which he is placed and he can set aside his right. However, another does not always have the opportune time for correction and he cannot set aside this good of another; therefore, he is bound to admonish his neighbor.[38]

While it is true that a sinner does not commit a sin of unrepentance if he does not repent immediately after a sin,[39] this fact does not release another from the obligation of fraternally correcting him. If one knows that the delinquent is in mortal sin and here and now so disposed to accept the correction, one may not put it off. Even if the sinner is prodigal in matters of his own spiritual welfare, another has to aid him when this spiritual need is present.[40] The argument of opponents to this opinion is aptly answered by St. Alphonsus. One can have a greater obligation towards others than to self. Thus, out of love for poverty, one need not relieve a grave personal temporal need to which he is subject; but another, who is rich, has the obligation to help him if he can.[41] In the case we are con-

---

[38] Suarez, *op. cit.* (disp. 8 sect. 3, n. 8). 12, 697.

[39] Merkelbach, *Summa Theologiae Moralis*, 3, 353.

[40] Ledesma, *Theologia Moralis* (tr. 4, c. 4). p. 194.

[41] *Theologia Moralis* (ed. Le Noir). I, 332: Cf., Salmanticensis Collegii, *Cursus Theologiae Moralis, de charitate* (c. 7, punct. 4, n. 49). 5, 154.

sidering we can help the delinquent and, even though the sinner has no obligation to return to grace immediately after sin, supposing the sinner's good will, we must correct him.

Before leaving the question of mortal sin, we must consider fraternal correction in relation to aiding a neighbor who has not sinned, but is in the proximate danger of falling into grave sin. There is considerable controversy on this point; but it is more a controversy on the application of *terms—lis de verbis—*rather than a controversy on the fact of a concrete obligation to give spiritual aid to a neighbor who is in the proximate danger of grave formal sin. All theologians are agreed that one is bound to give spiritual aid, at times, to one in such a condition; but whether or not this act of spiritual aid is specifically an act of fraternal correction is a matter of dispute.[42]

Theologians distinguish between danger of sin and occasion of sin. A danger of sin can be both internal, as an evil thought, and external, any person, place or thing constituting a concrete danger. An occasion of sin is any external circumstance which constitutes a danger of sin. The danger is the genus, while the occasion is a species of the genus.[43] Since there are many factors, such as natural frailty, passions, acquired habits, or special internal inclinations, of which we have no knowledge, here we will deal with the occasion of sin, inasmuch as it is a proximate danger of formal mortal sin for a neighbor. This is something external and thus, easily knowable and can be included in the object matter of fraternal correction.

We must make some necessary distinctions before entering into the question of correction relative to the proximate dangers of sin. There is an obligation for all to avoid the occasion of sin; but this obligation is not absolute, for con-

---

[42] *Cf.,* Sylvius, *Comm.* (II-II, q. 33, a. 2). 3, 164.; Catalanus, *Universi Juris* (pars 1, q. 7, c. 6). I, 168; Castropalao, *De Charitate* (disp. 2, punct. 2, n. 2). I, 441; Toletus, *Enarratio* (II-II, q. 33, a. 2). 2, 208; Salmanticensis Collegii, *op cit., de chartate* (c. 7, punct. 4 n. 50). 5, 154.

[43] G. De Varceno-S. Loiano, *Institutiones Theologiae Moralis,* I, 387.

crete obligations depend on various circumstances. An occasion of sin may be remote or proximate, depending on the degree of the danger of sin. Again theologians differ in their explanation of the proximate danger of sin. When there is *moral certitude* that this person, place, or thing, will lead to sin, all theologians are agreed that this constitutes a proximate danger of sin.[14] When the person, place, or thing will *probably* lead to sin, some theologians consider this as a proximate occasion. Thus, De Lugo holds that if an occasion frequently leads to sin, this occasion is to be considered as proximate.[15] For St. Alphonsus an *absolute proximate occasion* of sin would be present if it generally leads man into sin.[16] It can be held that a proximate occasion of sin is present if there is a solidly probable opinion that this occasion will lead to sin.

An absolute proximate occasion of sin is an occasion of sin for all men; a relative proximate occasion of sin is one that does not affect some men but for other individuals it constitutes a danger. An occasion of sin can be free or necessary; free, if the individual can easily abandon it; necessary, if it is either physically or morally impossible to get rid of the occasion.[17] It is the unanimous teaching of theologians that one is bound under the pain of mortal sin to avoid the free and proximate occasion of sinning gravely.[18] If the proximate occasion is a necessary one, for a just cause one can expose himself to the proximate danger of formal sin, when there is only a probable danger and when means are used to make this occasion remote. The latter case is but an application of the rule of double effect.[19]

We now enter the problem at hand: whether or not the act of giving spiritual aid to a neighbor who is in the

[14] *Ibid., loc. cit.*

[15] *Disputationes Scholasticae et Morales* (disp. 14, sect. 10, n. 149). 4, 654.

[16] *Theologia Moralis* (ed. Le Noir). 3, 371.

[17] Varceno-Loiano, *op. cit.,* I, 388-389.

[18] St. Alphonsus, *op. cit.,* 3, 374: *cf.,* Vermeersch, *Theologia Moralis,* 3, 480.

[19] Prümmer, *Manuale Theologiae Moralis,* I, 45; *cf.* Vermeersch, *op. cit., loc. cit.*

proximate danger of formal mortal sin is an obligation arising from the precept of fraternal correction? It is agreed that there is an obligation to give aid. Is it, however, to be considered as an obligation flowing from the precept of charitable correction, or is it an obligation arising from another source?

While we do not agree with Gregory of St. Vincent when he states that the theologians are unanimous in their teaching that future sin is matter for fraternal correction,[50] it certainly is the common opinion that, *in virtue of the precept of fraternal correction*, one is bound to correct a neighbor who is in the proximate danger of formal mortal sin. Basing themselves on the strict interpretation of the text of St. Matthew, Castropalao,[51] Sylvius,[52] De Coninck,[53] and St. Albert[54] hold that, although there is an obligation to give spiritual aid in the stated circumstance, this obligation does not come from the precept of fraternal correction. According to this opinion, since the neighbor has not sinned, he cannot be fraternally corrected. However, the Carmelite theologians of Salamanca,[55] Denis the Carthusian,[56] Gregory of St. Vincent,[57] Toletus,[58] Mastrio[59] and Babenstuber,[60] along with St. Alphonsus[61] and Billuart,[62] hold that this obligation arises from the precept of fraternal correction. While some of these authors do not hold this opinion explicitly, at least the notion of forestalling sin,

---

[50] *De Remediis Ignorantiae* (disp. 2, dub. 6, n. 14). p. 96.

[51] *De Charitate* (disp. 2, punct. 2, n. 2). I, 441.

[52] *Comm.* (II-II, q. 33, a 2, q. 4). 3, 166.

[53] *De Moralitate* (lib. 4, disp. 28, dub. 4). p. 573.

[54] *In Evang. Matthaei* (In Matt. 18:15). 20, 675.

[55] *Cursus Theologiae Moralis, de charitate* (c. 7, punct. 4, n. 50). 5, 154.

[56] *Summa De Vitiis et Virtutibus* (lib. 2, a. 41). 7, 229.

[57] *Op. cit.* (disp. 2, dub. 6, n. 14). p. 96.

[58] *Enarratio* (II-II, q. 33, a. 2). 2,208.

[59] *Theologia Moralis*, p. 293.

[60] *Ethica Supernaturalis Salisburgensis Sive Cursus Theologiae Moralis*, p. 315.

[61] *Theologia Moralis* (ed. Le Noir). I, 332.

[62] *Summa Sancti Thomae*, 3, 536.

when the neighbor is in the proximate danger of formal mortal sin, is included in their definitions of fraternal correction. These authors would seem to furnish at least an extrinsically probable opinion that this obligation is included in the precept of fraternal correction.

Despite the fact that St. Thomas seems to exclude this opinion from the meaning of the text,[63] sufficient authority is present for an extrinsically probable opinion. Along with the authors just quoted, the examples of fraternal correction given by St. Augustine and St. John Chrysostom seem to be dealing with the correction of a neighbor who is about to place himself in an absolute proximate danger of formal mortal sin.[64]

In the wide application of the term, admonition, given to one in the proximate danger of formal mortal sin, is an act of charitable correction; the obligation flowing from the precept of fraternal correction. Although this notion is not formally contained in the words of the precept, it is virtually present in the words of Christ; for it seems reasonable that an act be ascribed to the same precept, not only when there is actual necessity, but also, when one is in the circumstance which would bring about this necessity. Since correction in this case forestalls an actual danger, admonition here seems to be demanded by the precept of fraternal correction.

Closely allied to these objective considerations of the necessary matter for fraternal correction is the practical question of a neighbor's actual need. If the sinner has already returned to grace, there is no obligation to correct him.[65]

---

[63] *In Matthaeum Evangelistam Expositio*, c. 18: " . . . *peccaverit*: unde loquitur de peccato perpetrato. Unde aliter procedendum est in peccato perpetrato, aliter in perpetrando: quia perpetratum non potest esse non perpetratum. Unde in perpetrando est operam dare quod non fiat." *Cf.*, *De Correctione Fraterna*, a. 2 ad 10: "Dominus non loquitur de culpa futura cavenda, sed de culpa praeterita jam praecommissa."

[64] *Cf.*, *supra*, p. 85.

[65] Suarez, *De Charitate* (disp. 8, sect. 3, n. 7): " . . . si scio fratrem esse emendatum, absque occasione reincidendi, non teneor corripere, quia non eget." 12, 697; *cf.*, Salmanticensis Collegii, *op. cit.*, *de charitate* (c. 7, punct. 4, n. 49). 5, 154.

This obligation to correct is present only when one foresees that without it the sinner will remain in sin for a long time,[66] and also foresees that no other person will fulfill the duty and that there would be grave difficulty for the sinner to free himself from sin or from the occasion of sin.[67]

ARTICLE II

VENIAL AND MATERIAL SIN

The essential character of fraternal correction is plain; it is a charitable endeavor to aid a neighbor, who is in sin or in the proximate occasion thereof, to the attainment of eternal salvation. In the analysis of the ideas and in the observation of the facts considered up until now, stress was placed on the obligation one has to aid a neighbor in his grave or extreme spiritual necessity. Neither venial nor material sin brings about this necessity, for, by these, the soul is not deprived of divine life. Thus, if there is an obligation to correct a neighbor when he sins venially or when he is committing material sins, this obligation cannot be proved to exist on the grounds of grave or extreme spiritual necessity, for these are not present.

In the consideration of the text of St. Matthew, it was pointed out that our Blessed Lord was dealing with those sins which bring about grave or extreme spiritual necessity, for the object of this act is primarily mortal sin. Origen, on the other hand, restricts correction to venial sin, for he holds that if the sin is grave one ceases to be a brother.[68] The reason given for this restrictive interpretation is false, for sinners are not necessarily excluded from the body of

---

[66] Suarez, op. cit., loc. cit.

[67] Gregory of Valentia, *Commentaria Theologica, de charitate* (q. 10, punct. 2). 3, 816.

[68] *Commentaria in Evang. Secundum Matthaeum*, tom. 13, n. 30 (PG 13, 1174); cf., St. Augustine, *De Verbis Domini*, sermo 82, c. 4, n. 7 (PL 38, 508), where it is clear that, even though pagans are not to be considered as brothers, we have an obligation to correct those outside the fold, if we can help them.

the faithful.⁶⁹ We have already shown that *brother* is not to be understood only in the restrictive sense of fellow-believers.⁷⁰

It is evident that this obligation of correction primarily refers to the correction of formal mortal sin, but here we ask the question whether or not it is to be extended to venial and material sin. In order to arrive at a solution of this problem, theologians have introduced various distinctions in their treatment of the obligation of charitable correction relative to venial sin. All are in substantial agreement that one is bound to correct a neighbor, if the venial sin disposes to mortal. Navarrus,⁷¹ Bonacina,⁷² and Gregory of St. Vincent,⁷³ hold that there is an obligation of fraternal correction relative to venial sin, *only* if the sin disposes to mortal. They hold that *per se* there is no obligation but *per accidens*, by reason of the danger of falling into mortal sin, one is bound to correct a delinquent for this type of venial sin. An example of this would be present if one saw a friend going to a house where he engages in venially sinful conversation with a woman and this venially sinful conversation disposes him to commit mortal sin. Navarrus,⁷⁴ Catalanus⁷⁵ and Concina⁷⁶ hold that there would be a grave obligation to aid him by fraternal correction: Ledesma⁷⁷ and Bonacina⁷⁸ hold that the obligation would not be grave since, in the given case, there is no grave or extreme spiritual necessity. However, if this venial sin which disposes to mortal is considered as a proximate occasion of formal mortal sin, then the obligation would be grave.⁷⁹

⁶⁹ *Cf., Mystici Corpus Christi*, AAS 35 (1943), 203.

⁷⁰ *Cf., supra*, p. 43-45.

⁷¹ *Enchiridion Sive Manuale* (c. 24, n. 12). I, 440.

⁷² *Opera De Morali Theologia*, 2, 169.

⁷³ *De Remediis Ignorantiae* (disp. 2, dub. 6, n. 14). p. 94.

⁷⁴ *Op. cit., loc. cit.*

⁷⁵ *Universi Juris* (pars 1, q. 7, c. 6). I, 168.

⁷⁶ *Theologia Christiana*, I, 94.

⁷⁷ *Theologia Moralis* (tr. 4, c. 4). p. 195.

⁷⁸ *Op. cit., loc. cit.*

⁷⁹ Tanner, *Theologia Scholastica, de spe et charitate* (q. 5, dub. 4). 3, 684.

Suarez holds that there is an obligation to prevent venial sin when it is considered as a proximate occasion of grave sin, and it is a grave obligation, but he does not consider it as an act of fraternal correction.[80]

When there is question of simple venial sin, *i. e.*, venial sin which does not dispose to mortal, all theologians are agreed that there can be no grave obligation to forestall or correct the sinner. The gravity of the obligation depends on the matter; and where the matter is light, there can be no grave obligation.[81] If we can counsel one to commit a venial sin without committing a grave sin, *a fortiori* it cannot be a grave sin to omit correction for simple venial sin.[82]

The existence of a light obligation of charitable correction, relative to simple venial sin, is a matter of dispute. St. Albert the Great, taking sin in the strict meaning of the term, clearly excludes venial sin as object matter for this precept.[83] St. Bonaventure[84] and d'Aste[85] hold that the precept of fraternal correction deals with mortal sin, while the correction of venial sin is a matter of counsel. This distinction is perhaps due to the Scotistic teaching that the essence of venial sin consists in the fact that it is an act against a counsel, while the essence of mortal sin is found in the act contrary to a precept.[86] Michel,[87] Mastrio,[88] and Thomas of Charmes[89] also hold that the precept of fraternal correction does not extend to the correction of venial sin.

It is the more common opinion that one is obliged *sub levi* to correct a neighbor when he commits a simple venial

[80] *De Charitate* (disp. 8, sect. 3, n. 5).   12, 694.

[81] Merkelbach, *Summa Theologiae Moralis*, I, 434.

[82] Suarez, *op. cit.*, *loc. cit.*

[83] *In Evang. Matthaei* (In Matt. 18:15).   20, 675.

[84] *Compendium Theologicae Veritatis*, lib. 5, c. 70.   In Vives Edition of *Opera* (8, 202), not found in the Quarrachi Edition.

[85] *Summa Astensi* (lib. 2, tit. 67, a. 4).   I, 269.

[86] J. Scotus, *In II Sent.* (dist. 21, q. 1).   13, 137; *cf.*, Billuart, *Summa Sancti Thomae*, 2, 553.

[87] *Theologia Canonico-Moralis*, p. 403.

[88] *Theologia Moralis*, p. 293.

[89] *Theologia Universa ad usum Sacrae Theologiae Candidatorum*, 5, 114.

sin. Among the theologians holding this opinion are Cajetan,[90] Gregory of Valentia,[91] Bannez,[92] Ledesma,[93] and the
Carmelites of Salamanca.[94] The fact that our Lord deals
with grave sin, in the cited text of St. Matthew, does not
exclude this teaching that there is an obligation to correct
venial sin; for it is implicitly included in the precept.[95]

It is reasonable to suppose this obligation relative to
venial sin; for when a neighbor commits a venial sin, there
is some spiritual need, because venial sin, although it
does not deprive the soul of the life of grace, is a spiritual
deformity and impedes the reception of many graces. The
precept of love of neighbor commands that we love our
neighbor as ourselves. Our love of self must include the
avoidance of venial sin; and thus, we should endeavor to
remove this spiritual evil from our neighbor's life when
we can do so with little or no inconvenience. It is an obligation which binds *sub levi.*[96]

When treating of the question of fraternal correction
relative to material sin, theologians usually consider this
obligation in relation to those sins which are merely material because of the sinner's inculpable lack of knowledge.
The exact nature of material sin is not clearly developed
in the theological writings. Manualists, in general, define
material sin as "a transgression of the divine law caused by
invincible ignorance or by violence which destroys internal

---

[90] *Summula Cajetani,* (s. v. correctio). p. 127.

[91] *Commentaria Theologica, de charitate* (q. 10, punct. 2). 3,
822.

[92] *De Fide, Spe et Charitate* (q. 33, a. 2). p. 873.

[93] *Theologia Moralis* (tr. 4, c. 4). 195.

[94] *Cursus Theologiae Moralis, de charitate* (c. 7, punct. 4, n.
46). 5, 154.

[95] Castropalao, *De Charitate* (disp. 3, punct. 3, n. 4): "Fateor
Dominum (Matt. 18) locutum fuisse de correctione peccantis mor-
taliter, non venialiter. At non infertur non esse praeceptum de
corrigendo fratre peccanti venialiter in illo praecepto tacite inclus-
um, non quidem sub culpa gravi, sed levi." I, 442.

[96] *Ibid., loc. cit.; cf.* Suarez, *De Charitate* (disp. 8, sect. 3, n.
5). 12, 694.

consent."[97]   The early ecclesiastical writers recognised the fact that knowledge was a necessary condition for moral guilt. Thus, Tertullian shows that the deliberate consent of the will is necessary for moral guilt.[98]   In the teaching of St. Augustine, we find a clear affirmation that sin is a voluntary evil and, as a necessary condition, the evil must be known and embraced.[99]   For moral imputability, knowledge is so necessary that its absence either takes away sin or lessens its moral imputability. Abelard[100] seems to have introduced a distinction which later served as the basis for Peter Lombard's distinction between vincible and invincible ignorance.[101]   Peter of Poitiers gives us a clear basis for the distinction between formal and material sin when he points out that an act can be good or bad according to the disposition of the agent, while in itself it can have objective morality.[102]

Thus, when dealing with material sin, the act of the agent—*opus operantis*—is not sinful in the sense of moral imputability, for the formal aspect of sin, the voluntary transgression of law, is not present; but the material aspect of the act—*opus operatum*—is objectively contrary to God's law. From these distinctions, it is evident that material sin cannot, of itself, bring about a grave or extreme spiritual necessity, for it is not morally imputable. In the question of fraternal correction, when dealing with material sin, we consider the obligation of giving aid to a neighbor who sins

---

[97] Prümmer, *Manuale Theologiae Moralis,* "Peccatum . . . materiale . . . est transgressio legis divinae ex ignorantia invincibilis aut ex violentia internum consensum destruente." I, 244.

[98] *De Poenitentia,* c. 3 (PL I, 1232).

[99] *Retractationes,* lib. 1, c. 14, n. 4 (CSEL 36, 75 Knoell): " . . . peccatum sine voluntate esse non posse verissimum est . . . Nam et qui nesciens peccavit non incongruenter noles peccasse dici potest . . . "

[100] *Ethica,* c. 14 (PL 178, 657).

[101] *Libri Quatuor Sententiarum,* 2, dist. 22:   "Est enim ignorantia, quae excusat peccatum; et est talis ignorantia quae non excusat; est autem ignorantia invincibilis, et ignorantia vinciblis." p. 310.

[102] *Sententiae Petri Pictaviensis* (ed. P. Moore-M. Dulong). p. 156; *Cf., Sententiarum Libri,* lib. 1, c. 16, (PL 211, 863).

materially because of ignorance. When hope of amendment is present we must correct those whose sins are caused by vincible ignorance.[103] This is evident from the nature of the ignorance, for lack of knowledge is either *indirecta et per accidens voluntaria* or *directa et per se voluntaria,*[104] neither of which excuses from moral guilt. Vincible ignorrance does not excuse from moral imputability and the sin resulting from it is a formal sin and thus, matter for fraternal correction.

Theologians are agreed that one has to give some kind of aid to a neighbor when his invincible ignorance causes a violation of the natural or positive divine law,[105] unless there is danger that the material sins will thereby be rendered formal. *Per se* the violation of the natural law is an evil—an objective violation of the right order established by God. Even though the sin is not formal, the *opus operatum* is evil and to permit this, by the omission of charitable correction, would be sinful. The positive divine law, since it is God's free ordination of man to his supernatural End,[106] must be protected from violation even when the violation is due to ignorance.[107]

When invincible ignorance causes an objective violation of human law, theologians are not in agreement whether or not there is an obligation to forestall this objective evil. Gobat gives an example where one would be obliged to wake up a neighbor who falls asleep at Mass.[108] Ledesma, distinguishing between ignorance of the law and ignorance of a particular fact of the law, holds that one would be bound to give spiritual aid to a neighbor if he does not know the law, but if it is ignorance of a fact of law, prescending from scandal, there would be no obligation to admonish him.[109]

[103] Collegii Salmanticensis, *Cursus Theologiae Moralis, de charitate* (c. 7, punct. 4, n. 53). 5, 153.

[104] St. Thomas, *Summa Theologica*, I-II, q. 76, a 4.

[105] St. Alphonsus, *Theologia Moralis* (ed. Le Noir). I, 331.

[106] Merkelbach, *Summa Theologiae Moralis,* I, 267.

[107] Billuart, *Summa Sancti Thomae*, 3, 538.

[108] *Experientiae Theologico-Sacramentalis Explicatae* (tr. 5, cas. 11, n. 278). p. 457.

[109] *Theologia Moralis* (tr. 4, c. 4). p. 197.

St. Alphonsus, although admitting the probability of the opposite opinion which states that there is no obligation to instruct one when there is material violation of human law, holds that it is the common opinion that one is bound to correct in the case.[110] The Salmanticenses,[111] Navarrus,[112] Bannez,[113] and others hold that there is no obligation with regard to the material violation of human law, while Sylvester,[114] Gregory of St. Vincent,[115] Sylvius,[116] St. Alphonsus,[117] and D'Annibale[118] hold that one is bound to correct or at least admonish another about this material violation of human law, if there is hope of preventing the evil.

Most of the theologians consider the question of forestalling material violations of law in their tracts on fraternal correction. This does not mean that these authors are of the opinion that such spiritual aid is an act of fraternal correction. They are about equally divided on the nature of this act; some hold that such giving of spiritual aid flows from the precept of giving instruction to the ignorant,[119] while others hold that it is properly an act of fraternal correction that dispels this ignorance.[120] While it is not possible for us to resolve this question definitively, we are inclined to the opinion which holds that such an obligation is properly an obligation arising from the precept of fraternal correction.

It has been shown that the proper act of fraternal cor-

---

[110] *Theologia Moralis* (ed. Le Noir). I, 331.

[111] *Cursus Theologiae Moralis, de charitate* (c. 7, punct. 4, n. 53). 5, 155.

[112] *Enchiridion Sive Manuale* (c. 24, n. 12). I, 440.

[113] *De Fide, Spe et Charitate* (q. 33, a. 2). p. 874.

[114] *Summa Summarum* (s. v. correctio). I, 164.

[115] *De Remediis Ignorantiae* (disp. 2, dub. 6, n. 14). p. 96.

[116] *Comm.* (II-II, q. 33, a. 2, q. 5). 3, 166.

[117] *Op. cit.* (ed. Le Noir). I, 331. Cf., *Homo Apostolicus* (tr. 4, c. 2, punct. 3, n. 20). p. 80.

[118] *Summula Theologiae Moralis*, 2, 60.

[119] Suarez, *De Charitate* (disp. 8, sect. 3, n. 6). 12, 694.

[120] St. Alphonsus, *Theologia Moralis* (ed. Le Noir). I, 331. Cf., *Homo Apostolicus* (tr. 4, c. 2, punct. 3, n. 20). p. 80.

rection is directed to the removal of the neighbor's sin inasmuch as the sin is considered as an evil to the sinner himself. Ignorance, although invincible, is an evil to the sinner himself; and if we can remove this ignorance, there seems to be an obligation to do so from the general precept of charitable correction. For example, when there is ignorance of the fundamental truths of Faith, this is an evil for the "sinner," for without knowledge of these truths salvation is impossible. Often the violation of law caused by ignorance is an evil to the "sinner," for, although here and now he sins only materially, there is a proximate danger or occasion of falling into formal sin. This is so because a habit may be formed; and after knowledge of the sinfulness of the act, because of a contracted habit, he will find it very difficult to give up that which he now knows to be morally evil. This seems to be the most forceful reason why he should be corrected. *Per accidens*, there would also be an obligation to correct the one who sins materially when there is danger of scandal.

Gregory of St. Vincent, in his classical tract *On the Remedies of Ignorance,* lists fraternal correction as one of the chief remedies.[121] Suarez, when treating of the confessor's obligation to give instruction to one who sins materially, shows that the confessor has a greater obligation than the one who is bound to instruct a material sinner in virtue of the precept of fraternal correction.[122] However, elsewhere he holds that this obligation of spiritual aid to one who sins materially, is an obligation flowing from the precept of giving counsel, and he explicitly states that it is not fraternal correction.[123] Denis the Carthusian gives us

---

[121] *De Remediis Ignorantiae* (disp. 2, dub. 6, n. 14). pp. 96-97.

[122] *De Poenitentia,* disp. 32, sect. 4, n. 3: " . . . ex charitate tenemur admonere proximum etiamsi ignoranter faciat id quod ex se peccatum est, quando est spes fructus, ut constat ex materia de Correctione Fraterna; quia haec ipsa ignorantia et hujusmodi status est magnum malum proximi, et ideo ipsa ratio misericordiae obligat ad subveniendum illi, quando est spes fructus, juxta generales regulas misericordiae." 22, 680.

[123] *De Charitate,* disp. 8, sect. 3, n. 6: "Et simili modo expeditur aliud dubium, an si opus fratris sit de se peccatum mortale, ille

a good reason why such instruction flows from the precept of fraternal correction.[124]

ARTICLE III

PRACTICAL APPLICATION OF PRINCIPLES

Before entering upon an application of the principles relative to the obligation of fraternal correction, one may well point out again the various conditions for a concrete obligation and also those circumstances in which one is released from the obligation. Briefly, the required conditions are four:

1) One must be sure that a neighbor is committing sin, either formal or material, or is in the proximate danger of sin.

2) There must be a reasonable hope of effecting some good by the charitable correction.

3) There must be little or no hope that a neighbor, if left to himself, will correct himself.

4) There must be no one else more fitting or equally apt to give this correction, and who will, in reality, carry it out.

From these general conditions, one may deduce those particular circumstances which excuse from the obligation in a concrete case. These are also four in number:

autem excusetur a culpa propter ignorantiam invincibilem, tenear corripere. Respondetur enim praeceptum spiritualis misericordiae proximi posse habere locum in tali materia . . . sed non esse tam correctionis, quam dandi consilii vel doctrinae . . . quia proximus ibi non delinquit neque periit." 12, 694.

[124] *In IV Sent.*, dist. 19, q. 1: "Omnis peccans excidit ab intellectu et sequitur partem irrationalem, ideo correctio seu correptio est admonitio, ut peccans ad lucem redeat intellectum qui regit viam juris." 24, 528.

1) If our correction will prove inefficacious, or perhaps make the sinner worse, we are excused from the obligation, unless, by the omission of our correction, the common good or the good of another will be endangered.

2) If there is a reasonable hope that the sinner will soon correct himself, our obligation ceases.

3) When one has knowledge that another will correct the sinner, there is no need of correction by the one who prudently judges that correction will be carried out by another, as for example by a parent or by a superior.

4) Outside the case of extreme spiritual necessity, if one foresees some grave harm to himself resulting from the correction, the obligation ceases.

We now can turn to a practical application of these principles.

Case 1:

The prudent and spiritually alive are often called upon to aid a neighbor who is a spiritual 'pauper.' United in a bond of spiritual solidarity, one has the obligation to provide for the spiritual wants of a neighbor. We often find joy in the supernatural goods which our neighbor possesses actually, but we are also bound to desire that he possess or receive those supernatural goods which he lacks. Primarily, we must wish that our neighbor possess God, here in this life by grace and hereafter in the glory of the Beatific Vision. But our well-wishing must be effective and we must activate it by taking the practical steps in helping him acquire these goods, insofar as it is possible. The omission of attendance at Sunday Mass is an evil for our neighbor, for, if one does not have a sufficient reason for not attending Mass on a day prescribed by the law, it is a mortal sin. If one knows that a friend misses Mass on Sunday without a sufficient reason, there can be an obligation to admonish him and to remind him of his duty.[125]   However, the conditions already mentioned would have to be verified. Thus, if it is only rumored that a neighbor does not attend Mass, there would be no obligation to correct him for moral certitude of the fault would not be present. Certain knowledge of the fault alone would not be a sufficient basis for the obligation of charitable correction, but when there is sufficient reason for prudently judging that the sinner will heed the correction, one should admonish the sinner about the gravity of his obligation to attend Mass. It may be difficult for the sinner to reform, if left to himself, either because he does not realize the seriousness of his condition, or he may be in a habit of acting in this manner from which it would be difficult for him to free himself, unless admonished and corrected by others. However, if one foresees that this reminder of the obligation will cause the sinner to blaspheme, correction must be omitted since this would be an added injury to the sinner. When another will correct him, and we have knowledge of this fact, there is no obligation to correct him.

Case 2:

It often happens that after a mortal sin, one is not in the danger of relapse but one does not repent and thus remains in sin for a long time. While some of the theologians hold that there is no obligation to remind the sinner of his sin in the case, we have held that it is the more probable opinion that one has to give correction given the proper circumstances.[126] Since the sinner is deprived of the life of grace by mortal sin, he is in grave spiritual necessity. While it is true that the sinner does not have an obligation to repent immediately after a fall into sin, if one sees that his amendment here and now can be effected by a charitable rebuke, it cannot be omitted without sin. Thus, if we know that a neighbor has committed a grave sin, as for example by using alcoholic liquors so as to cause a total 'black-out,' but has not yet gone to confession or has not yet made an act of perfect contrition, we know that he is

[125] Sylvius, *Comm.* (II-II, q. 33, a. 2, q. 5). 3, 167.
[126] Cf., *supra*, p. 89-92.

in the state of aversion from God. Since the time is opportune for correction—supposing his will to be corrected here and now—we must charitably correct him by reminding him of his status before God. However, if we see that a parent will correct him, our obligation ceases.

Case 3:

The ecclesiastical law forbids mixed marriages and they are also forbidden by divine law if there is a danger of perverting the Catholic party or the offspring of such a marriage.[127] One would be guilty of grave sin by keeping company with a non-catholic if there is reason to believe that there is no justifying reason for entering this marriage and especially when one is sure that the non-catholic will not keep the promise that all children will be brought up as Catholics. It is a mortal sin for a Catholic to enter a mixed marriage without a just and grave cause, consequently it is sinful to wish or plan such a marriage.[128] The Code of Canon Law obliges the Bishops and pastors of souls to deter Catholics from mixed marriages.[129] It also can be imposed as an obligation on the simple faithful to deter such marriages, when they know that there is little or no hope of a justifying reason for this marriage. Often the indirect method of correction will prove more efficacious than the direct. Instead of telling Catholics they are doing wrong, it will often be more fruitful to introduce them to suitable partners who offer no danger to faith. Often the complaint is that a Catholic has to seek such marriages with non-catholics because there is no opportunity to meet suitable Catholic partners. It would be an effective means of correction and a most charitable act to see that this person has an opportunity to meet with others of the faith.

Case 4:

A growing tendency is causing alarm among priests and parents alike. The students in the early years of high school

---

[127] *Can.* 1060.
[128] Merkelbach, *Summa Theologiae Moralis*, 3, 878.
[129] *Can.* 1064, n. 1.

are "going steady." Although the youngsters of fourteen or fifteen may not realize it, they are running the risk of exposing themselves to the proximate danger of grave sin. This frequent and exclusive companionship often leads to sins against the virtue of purity. It is a solid principle of moral theology that one cannot "keep company" or "go steady" unless marriage is planned within a reasonable time.[130] It is evident that these youngsters are not planning marriage and, thus, this "going steady" is objectively a mortal sin. Often parents look upon this exclusive companionship as something innocent and thus fail to correct their children on this point. Often the friends of the one who so exposes himself to danger can correct them by showing them the folly and the danger in such "closed-associations." They can prudently judge that if the attention of their friend is called to the danger, these associations will be broken off.

Case 5:

There can be little doubt that Catholics, in general, know the malice of birth control or contraception. But, Fr. Bertke, in his doctoral dissertation states that, due to the prevalence of propaganda in favor of contraception, some Catholics "may think birth control is not so bad after all, or at least they may reason that the malice of the sin under the circumstance would not be grave."[131] Although Cappello holds that a confessor would not be obliged to disturb the good faith of these people,[132] Merkelbach[133] and Iorio[134] hold that a confessor *regularly* must admonish the sinner about the evil of this practice, notwithstanding the lack of hope of successful correction. In practice, it often happens that a friend hears his Catholic neighbor extol birth control in such a way that there is little doubt that

[130] *Cf.*, F. Connell, "Adolescent Company Keeping," *The American Ecclesiastical Review*, 105, 6 (Dec. 1946). 458-459.

[131] *The Possibility of Invincible Ignorance of the Natural Law*, p. 98.

[132] *De Sacramentis*, 3, 872. In his later edition of *De Matrimonio* (Turin: Marietti, 1947), Cappello holds that it would be better to admonish such people of the evil of this practice. 5, 816.

[133] *Summa Theologiae Moralis*, 3, 962

[134] *Theologia Moralis*, 3, 671.

he is engaged in this evil practice. If there is no reasonable hope of effecting a conversion, or if we feel that we will make the sinner worse by correcting him—as for example, by making material sin a formal sin—the question of fraternal correction is not clear. It has been pointed out that if there is no hope of beneficial correction, or if the correction would cause one to commit a formal sin, where there was only material sin before the admonition—the obligation relative to the instruction of those who sin because of invincible ignorance—St. Alphonsus holds that one cannot be left in good faith if the action causes harm to the common good.[135] It has also been shown that a private individual cannot omit correction if the omission would be injurious to an other or would harm the common good.[136] Contraception is opposed to the common good and, thus, on general principles, the confessor must instruct the one who sins materially in this matter but in very exceptional cases one can leave the penitent in good faith.[137] The same principle can be applied, *a fortiori*, to the lawfulness of the omission of fraternal correction in this case. Even though contraception is against the common good, if there is no hope of turning one from this evil practice, correction, arising from the precept of charitable correction, may be omitted. If, however, scandal is given by this omission, we must correct even though there is no hope of effecting the good of the one practicing it; for, then, we have an obligation to prevent scandal when we can.

Case 6:

When a person is in the proximate danger of sinning gravely, as for example by visiting one with whom he frequently sins, if a neighbor knows that he can deter a friend from this occasion he is bound in charity to do so. While some theologians do not admit such an obligation of correction, it has been shown that the common opinion of theologians is that there is an obligation of detering a

---

[135] *Theologia Moralis* (ed. Le Noir). 3, 532.
[136] *Cf., supra*, p. 79.
[137] *Cf.,* Merkelbach, *op. cit.*, 3, 963.

neighbor from the proximate occasion of sin in virtue of the precept of fraternal correction[138] However, one must be sure that there is a proximate occasion of grave sin and that one will benefit by such a correction.

Case 7:

Even when there is no hope of effecting the conversion of the one who is doing great moral harm in a school or religious community, correction must be given by way of denunciation to the superior for this is but a means of protecting the common good. This could be verified in the case where one student is leading others to sin against the virtue of purity and there is danger to the spiritual good of others in the school. Of course, if the harm is limited to a few, one would not be obliged to go to any great inconvenience in order to denounce the sinner,[139] but in general it may be stated that one has a grave obligation to make the condition known to the proper authorities so that the evil may be checked and rooted-out.[140]

Case 8:

It is admitted that some kind of spiritual aid—either correction or admonition—must be given to those whose act is only a material violation of the natural and positive divine law. Thus, if there is reasonable hope of effecting some good, as for example, preventing this violation of the order established by God, admonition, correction or instruction should be given. If, for example, one knows that his neighbor is about to enter an invalid marriage because of the existence of a diriment impediment, this fact of an impediment must be made known to him, if there is hope that the violation, even though an inculpable violation, of the law can be averted.[141] If the marriage has already taken place and there is no hope that the man will leave his

[138] *Cf., supra*, p. 94.
[139] Noldin, *Summa Theologiae Moralis*, 2, 114.
[140] Billuart, *Summa Sancti Thomae*, 3, 543.
[141] *Ibid.*, 3, 538.

supposed wife, they must be left in good faith.[142]   The main reason why we should correct one who sins materially is that this act, while now a material sin, can constitute a proximate danger of formal sin.   Supposing a man does not know of his obligation to attend Sunday Mass, after years of missing Mass he will be in a habit and it will be most difficult for him to rid himself of the habit after knowledge is obtained of the Sunday precept.   The same may be said of sins against the virtue of purity.   Even though here and now there is a material violation, after a habit has been formed it will be hard to break it.   So if there is a reasonable hope that our correction will be effective and not turn material sin into formal sin, we must, in charity and in virtue of the precept of fraternal correction, admonish the "sinner."

Case 9:

When dealing with mere ecclesiastical laws, it can be stated that there is no obligation to correct non-catholics for their inculpable violation of ecclesiastical law.   That they are subject to the laws of the Church is now the common teaching of theologians and canonists for by Baptism a person becomes subject to the Church.[143]   However, since there would be little hope of their fulfilling the law because they would not admit the basis for the obligation, correction of non-catholics, in matters of ecclesiastical law, can be lawfully omitted.   We would be bound to correct them for a material and formal violation of natural and positive divine law only when there is reasonable hope of beneficial correction.

Case 10:

While a person who eats meat at a ball game on Friday, not realising that it is Friday, is not guilty of formal sin, one would have an obligation to admonish him of this fact if there were danger of giving scandal.   Ledesma gives

---

[142] *Ibid., loc. cit.*
[143] *Can.* 87.

what perhaps may be a safe opinion to follow; if a neighbor does not know the law, there is an obligation to correct him; if there is ignorance of a fact of law, as for example one forgets that it is Friday, there is no obligation to correct provided that there is no danger of scandal.[134] The reason for this distinction is clear; in the inadvertent breaking of the law, there is no danger of forming a habit, while, if one is ignorant of the law itself, repeated violations will form a habit and when the habit is not checked by correction or instruction, it will be hard for the person to avoid formal sin after knowledge of its malice is obtained.

[134] *Theologia Moralis* (tr. 4, c. 4). p. 197.

CHAPTER IV

THE EXCELLENCE AND EFFECTS OF FRATERNAL CORRECTION

A. The Excellence of Fraternal Correction

The excellence of the act of love which is directed to the spiritual well-being of our fellowman is clearly brought home to us in the writing of the Fathers and theologians. Pseudo-Denis, the Areopagite, teaches that among all things the most divine is to cooperate with God in the conversion of sinners.[1] St. John Chrysostom, speaking of the excellence of the act of love of neighbor, clearly states that this care of our neighbor's spiritual welfare pertains to the essence of Christianity.[2] He holds that, when our Lord gave the Apostles the mission of teaching all nations, this mission was given to all,[3] and there cannot be a Christian so cold who would not have the spiritual welfare of his neighbor at heart.[4] We are true Christians, he holds, when, in imitation of Christ, we give succor to a neighbor in a spiritual need.[5] No one can neglect the eternal salvation of a neighbor.[6] Commenting on this general obligation, St. John Chrysostom applies the words of Jeremias[7] to those who endeavor to lead a neighbor to the path of virtue.[8]

This general excellence of the spiritual works of mercy may be applied to fraternal correction, for, as St. Augustine

---

[1] De Coelesti Hierarchia, c. 3, 2 (PG 3, 166).

[2] In Act. Apost., hom. 29, 4 (PG 60, 163-164): "Alios inducere ad Christum pertinet ad essentiam Christianismi."

[3] In 2 Thesal., c. 3, hom. 5, n. 4 (PG 62, 498).

[4] In Act. Apost., hom. 29, 4 (PG 60, 162).

[5] In 1 Cor., hom. 25, 3 (PG 61, 208).

[6] Adversus Judaeos, c. 7, 6 (PG 48, 925).

[7] Jeremias 15:19 " . . . if thou wilt separate the precious from the vile, thou shalt be as my mouth."

[8] In Genes., hom. 3 (PG 53, 36-37).

113

tells us, if we fail to correct a neighbor when he sins, we do not love him.[9] It is true that "there is no sacrifice more agreeable to God than zeal for the salvation of souls."[10] Fraternal correction is manifestly a work of spiritual zeal for we, as far as possible in cooperation with God's grace, prevent a neighbor from losing his immortal soul. St. Thomas gives three reasons for the excellence of the spiritual works of mercy, showing that they are superior to the corporal works of mercy:

> First, indeed, because that which is offered is more excellent, since it is a spiritual gift, which surpasses a corporal gift . . . Secondly, because of the object on which the benefit is conferred, because the soul is more excellent than the body . . . Thirdly, as regards the acts themselves by which a neighbor is benefited, because spiritual acts are more excellent than the corporal which are, in some way, servile.[11]

Expressly, he holds that fraternal correction is an act of charity preferable to the cure of bodily infirmity and superior to almsgiving by which a bodily need is relieved.[12]

Having care for the spiritual welfare of our neighbor is but an external manifestation of our love of God and neighbor. Besides the motive of charity, when we cause others to participate in the spiritual gifts we have received from God, we also show our gratitude to Him. This notion is brought out in the works of St. John Chrysostom for he shows that by our act to lead others away from sin, we are

[9] *Tract. In Epist. Joannis ad Parthos.* 7, c. 4, 11 (PL 35, 2034-2035): "Non putes tunc te amare servum tuum . . . aut tunc te amare vicinum tuum, quando eum non corripis; non est ista charitas, sed languor. Ferveat charitas ad corrigendum, ad emendandum; sed si sunt boni mores delectent; si sunt mali, emendentur, corrigantur . . . "

[10] St. Gregory the Great, *Hom. in Ezech.*, lib. 1, hom. 12, 30 (PL 76, 932): "Nullum quippe omnipotenti Deo tale est sacrificium, quale est zelus animarum."

[11] *Summa Theologica*, II-II, q. 32, a. 3.

[12] *Ibid.*, II-II, q. 33, a. 1.

manifesting our gratitude for the redemptive work of Christ.[13]

B. *The Effects of Fraternal Correction*

In the formulation of principles, relative to the effects of fraternal correction, a twofold question may be asked: what effect does fraternal correction have on the sinner and what effect does it have on the one giving the correction?

In the time of St. Augustine, the Pelagians denied the necessity of grace for the efficacy of fraternal correction, while others held that fraternal correction was useless, for, without God's grace, it could not bring about the sinner's amendment.[14] These objections were answered by St. Augustine.[15] Since we do not know whether or not a man is called, predestined by grace, correction must be employed by all to those who stand in apparent need of it. Rebuke and grace are not contradictory.[16] The fact that a man's return to grace is effected by God's grace does not release us from the obligation, given the proper circumstances.

The relation of fraternal correction to a man's conversion to grace is an important question; the solution of which will lead to a better understanding of the effectiveness of this act. God uses many means in the conversion of sinners; and although these means, such as preaching and correction, do not confer grace, God has so ordained the conversion of some sinners that these will not be converted unless these means are employed. We do not know what particular means God has ordained for the conversion of our neighbor, so, given the circumstance of spiritual need in which fraternal correction may be applied, we must correct.[17] How-

[13] *In Genes.*, hom. 3 (PG 53, 37).

[14] *Cf.*, Suarez, *De Charitate* (disp. 8, sect. 1). 12, 692.

[15] *De Correptione et Gratia*, (PL 44, 915-946).

[16] *Ibid.*, c. 14, 43 (PL 44, 942).

[17] Sylvius, *Comm.*, II-II, q. 33, a. 2: "Etsi homo per correptionem non conferat gratiam, Deus tamen eo ipsius actu vult uti, ut aliquos peccatores convertat. Implendae enim voluntatis Dei erga peccatorum conversionem ita est praeordinatur effectus ut quosdam non convertat nisi adhibita praedictorum diligentia; cateros non nisi adjuncta fratris correctione privata; alios aliter. Et quia ignotum est nobis quo medio velit Deus hunc fratrem corrigere, debemus ea adhibere quae ipse praescribit." 3, 164.

ever, it must be remembered that our correction is not the *cause* of grace, but it can be an occasion in which grace is given our neighbor. God has prescribed this act of love; its fulfillment is an act of obedience to the Will of God, and it can be the means by which God desires that His Will, in relation to the conversion of sinners, be carried out for:

> these are so called in one way, those in another and others still in another way, according to the different and innumerable ways, wherefore be it far from us to assert that it is the business of the clay [i. e. man] to judge, but it is the business of the potter [i. e. God].[18]

True love of God is not idle; it seeks to fulfill the Will of the Loved one. The Christian, actuated by and on fire with the love of God, by fraternally correcting a delinquent can be the occasion disposing the sinner to accept God's grace. The ultimate effectiveness of the act of love depends on God, for:

> When men either come or return to the way of justice by means of rebuke, who is it that works salvation in their hearts, but that God who gives the increase to those who plant and water, and who labor in the fields and shrubs.[19]

Here, St. Augustine compares the one who gives fraternal correction to the laborer who tills the field. The symbolism is apparent; for, by our correction, we render a man's heart susceptible to God's grace by removing the thorns and briars which impede man's conversion to grace. Overcome by passion and ignorance, man often finds it difficult to return to virtue; so, by fraternally correcting him, we show him the evil of his ways. The act of love indicates to a neighbor those thorns and briars of sin which make him less willing to accept God's grace. We but point out the way of

---

[18] St. Augustine, *op. cit.*, c. 5, 8 (PL 44, 920).

[19] *Ibid.*, c. 14, n. 43 (PL 44, 942).

virtue; the return to grace depends on our neighbor's cooperation with the grace God gives him.

Fraternal correction is not of itself effective of conversion for conversion is the work of God. Although the natural cannot positively dispose to the supernatural, correction is an effective means in pointing out the malice of sin and thus disposes—by the removal of obstacles—for the reception of grace. It is an external grace given by God through our instrumentality. While it is beyond the scope of this dissertation to go into the distinction between internal and external actual grace, it can be safely maintained that fraternal correction may be classified as a *gratia actualis externa*, for, even though it does not internally move the intellect and will, like preaching it suggests the way of return to virtue. Pelagius' doctrine on the efficacy of fraternal correction without grace stems from the fact that he admitted the sufficiency of merely external grace. St. Augustine shows that internal grace is necessary for the efficacy of fraternal correction and it can come only from God.[20] Without an internal actual grace, a man in mortal sin cannot come to recognition of his condition and cannot come to a firm resolution to return to God unless this internal inspiration of grace be present.[21]

Before dealing with the effects which this charitable act has on the donor, it must be recalled here that charitable correction has been defined as:

> any prudent word or deed, springing from the virtues of charity and mercy, by which one prudently attempts to procure a neighbor's personal spiritual good by turning him from sin and from the proximate occasion of sin.[22]

It has been pointed out that mercy, although a special virtue—having as its own formal object the relief of another's need out of compassion—is the proper effect of charity.

---

[20] *De Gratia et Libero Arbitrio*, c. 17, n. 33 (PL 44, 901).
[21] Cf., *Concilium Tridentinum* (Sess. 6, can. 3). DUB 812.
[22] Cf., *supra*, p. 23.

We have considered the supernatural motive of love of neighbor, showing that we love a neighbor for God's sake. Our affective love of neighbor, leads to an effective love. By our love of desire, we wish that our neighbor may receive those supernatural goods which he lacks; and we put this affective desire into effective action by helping, as far as we can, in the attainment of these spiritual goods by turning our neighbor from sin or from the proximate occasion of formal sin. This is real love of our neighbor for God's sake.

It is clear that one who is in the state of grace, merits an increase of grace by fraternally correcting a neighbor, for all the conditions for supernatural merit are present.[23] We are performing a voluntary good which is supernatural and God has promised a reward to those who fulfill His Will. The motive of this act is supernatural. It would take us too far afield to go into the question of what influence of charity is required to make an act meritorious. Some hold that ethically good acts performed by one in the state of grace merit an increase of grace.[24] Others hold that the act must be at least virtually prompted by charity.[25] St. Thomas gives a practical solution to this problem when he states that "there cannot be any act proceeding from the free will of one having grace, which is not meritorious."[26] Here, in dealing with the question of fraternal correction, since the act proceeds from charity *actually*, we can state that this act performed by a man in the state of grace does merit an increase of grace.

We have already pointed out that even a sinner has an obligation to correct another delinquent.[27] An interesting question may be raised relative to the effect this act of love has on the sinner who corrects. Theologians do not go into details on this question, so whatever conclusion reached here has to be based on the general principles stated by theological writers. We have indicated a passage

[23] Prümmer, *Manuale Theologiae Moralis*, I, 94.
[24] *Ibid.*, I, 95.
[25] St. Bonaventure, *In II Sent.* (dist. 41, a. 1, q. 3). 13, 435.
[26] *In II Sent.*, dist. 40, q. 1, a. 5.
[27] *Cf., supra*, p. 35.

from the teaching of St. Augustine where it is clear that
an act of mercy is not only of obligation for the sinner but
also profitable.[28] Cajetan also points out that the sinner can
profit by this act of correction[29] while Daelman states that
both spiritual and corporal almsgiving, motivated by charity, have a supernatural effect. He holds that these acts,
performed by one in the state of grace, merit an increase
of grace; if performed by one who is not in the state of
grace under the influence of actual grace, other actual graces
will be merited *de congruo.*[30]

We read in the Book of Daniel "redeem thou thy sins
with alms."[31] St. Thomas shows two ways in which a man
can be liberated from mortal sin by almsgiving; it impedes
future mortal sin and disposes one in sin to recover grace.[32]
However, almsgiving does not *per se* and infallibly take
away mortal sin; neither *ex opere operato* as do the sacraments, nor *ex opere operantis* as does love of God *super
omnia.* But *per accidens,* because of a definite relation to
charity, when one aids a neighbor actuated by the love of
God *super omnia* almsgiving infallibly removes mortal sin.[33]

The question then resolves itself to this: can the act of
fraternal correction, being a work of spiritual alms, sanctify
the sinner when he is in a state of aversion from God? It
is certain that a man in mortal sin can merit *de congruo*
other actual graces and even sanctifying graces.[34] The
solution of the question resolves around the motive. If,

[28] *Cf., supra,* p. 37.
[29] *Comm.* in II-II, q. 33, a. 5.
[30] *De Charitate* (q. 9, obs. 10). 4, 311.
[31] Daniel 4:24.
[32] *In IV Sent.,* dist, 15, q. 3, a. 2: " . . . eo modo quo aliquis
liberatur a peccato mortali per eleemosynam, liberatur ab inferna-
libus tenebris. Liberat autem eleemosyna a peccato hominem
adhuc in statu viae existentem dupliciter: vel impediendo futurum peccatum . . . vel a praeterito liberando in quantum disponit
eum qui in peccatum incidit, ad gratiam recuperandam, sicut et
alia opera de genere bonorum recta intentione facta."
[33] Sporer, *Theologia Moralis* (tr. 3, c. 6, sect. 2, n. 37). I, 464.
[34] Prümmer, *Manuale Theologiae Moralis,* I, 97.

under the influence of actual grace, one gives spiritual aid to a neighbor who is in sin or in the proximate occasion of sin, mortal sin will be removed from the donor's soul by fraternally correcting a neighbor *if* the act is motivated by supernatural love of God *super omnia*. Unlike the corporal works of mercy, which are often merely acts of natural benevolence, fraternal correction is more apt to be undertaken from this superior motive of charity.

It is the common theological teaching that love of God because He is all good in Himself is perfect love of God. In this love there is a preference for God above all created things. It has been shown above that the principle and end of our supernatural love of neighbor is God and that supernatural love of neighbor is not a virtue distinct from charity towards God, but rather a specification of the material object of charity. Pity or mercy leads to charity; but *in se* it is not a theological virtue. It is a moral virtue whose motive springs from the reasonableness inherent in the act of relieving another's distress. It is evident then, that if this reasonableness is the *sole* motive for fraternally correcting a delinquent, this does not sanctify the one correcting, for the motive which characterizes perfect love of God is not present. If we correct a neighbor, however, because of a detestation for sin founded on the motive that sin is an offense against God Who is loved above all else, evidently, we have placed, under the influence of actual grace, an act of perfect love of God which sanctifies. This supernatural act, placed by the sinner, has to be placed under the influence of actual grace; for it would not be supernatural unless this specific supernatural power were given him to enable the soul to place this act. The supernatural motive of this act is to be found in the fact that we correct a neighbor because sin is against the Infinite Goodness of God. We love our neighbor *propter Deum*: for his real or potential participation of the Divine Goodness. When one corrects a neighbor, he is exercising an act of love of neighbor and consequently an act of love for God. It is true that the motive of correction is directly ordained to the spiritual good of a neighbor, but this does not exclude the motive of an act of perfect love. Sin can be considered as an evil to a neighbor and also as an offense against the

Infinite Goodness of God. Thus, when motivated by a love of God *super omnia,* when one corrects a neighbor he manifests zeal for the glory of God and this is an act of charity.[35] Charity and mortal sin are mutually exclusive, for an act of charity destroys mortal sin and justifies the sinner.

Thus, the particular spiritual effect of fraternal correction on the sinner who corrects another delinquent may be twofold; correction is a means of meriting *de congruo* other actual graces and *per accidens*—if it is motivated by a supernatural love of God *super omnia*—it can bring about the sanctification of the one correcting. It can also inspire the sinner with such hate for sin, that, under the influence of actual grace, he is apt to place an act of perfect contrition, which also justifies.

[35] St. Thomas, *Summa Theologica,* I-II, q. 28, a. 4.

CONCLUSION

Fraternal correction, an obligation of natural and positive divine law, is any word or deed, motivated by the virtues of charity and mercy under the direction of prudence, which attempts to procure a personal spiritual good for a neighbor by turning him from sin or from the proximate occasion of sin. It is not restricted to the correction of a personal fault against us but it attempts to remove all sin from a neighbor's life. It is a proper remedy for sins of negligence or passion which have been committed, but it also can be extended to the prevention of sin when a neighbor is in the proximate occasion of sin. While this act of love is directed to the protection of the eternal salvation of another and, thus, deals properly with the correction of mortal sins, it is probable that venial and material sins must be corrected in virtue of the precept of charitable correction. This obligation of giving such spiritual aid is a grave obligation but it can admit lightness of matter and at times the omission of correction is a virtuous act. All men, even sinners, are subject to this law of giving spiritual aid to a neighbor who is a delinquent.

Being an act arising from an affirmative precept, this obligation is binding only in certain circumstances. Thus, before there is a concrete obligation, we must be reasonably sure that the delinquent is willing to accept correction; for, if there is no hope of beneficial correction, this act of fraternal love will defeat its own purpose. The one correcting should have moral certitude of the fact of sin or of the fact that a neighbor is in the proximate occasion of sinning gravely. Private individuals should not inquire into the life of another in order to find something which needs correction. The mere fact that one knows that another is a sinner and not in the state of grace does not always oblige one to give correction, even though he knows his correction will be beneficial, for one could foresee that a parent or another better suited for the task will correct.

Prudence, which governs the exercise of virtue, is particularly necessary here in the fulfillment of this obligation.

At times, due to particular circumstances, the omission of fraternal correction can be meritorious, as when we foresee that a delinquent, by our correction, would become worse. Prudence directs us to be secret about the correction and private correction is a matter of precept. However, when the common good or the good of a third person demand it, denunciation can be resorted to without any previous private admonition, but this is an exceptional case.

If our neighbor is in extreme spiritual necessity, no temporal consideration will excuse us from the non-fulfillment of the obligation, given all the circumstances especially certainty that the correction will be accepted. When there is only grave spiritual necessity, while we are bound to go to some inconvenience to fulfill the obligation, if its fulfillment would mean some serious harm or damage for us we would be excused from the obligation. No mathematical rules can be given but prudence must direct us in giving or omitting fraternal correction.

If this obligation is fulfilled by one in the state of grace, an increase of grace will be merited; if performed by a sinner in the state of aversion from God, he will merit other graces *de congruo;* if his act is motivated by a love of God *super omnia,* the sinner will be justified.

BIBLIOGRAPHY

Sources

Acta Apostolicae Sedis, Commentarium Officiale, (AAS), Romae: Typis Polyglottis Vaticanis, 1909-.

Codex Juris Canonici Pii X Pontificis Maximi jussu digestus, Benedicti Papae XV auctoritate promulgatus, (CJC), Romae: Typis Polyglottis Vaticanis, 1936.

Corpus Scriptorum Ecclesiasticorum Latinorum, (CSEL), editum consilio et impensis Academiae Litterarum Caeserea Vindobonensis, Vienna, 1866-.

Decretum Gratiani Emendatum et Notationibus Illustratum una cum glossis Gregorii XIII Pontificis Maximi jussu editum, 3 vols., Turin, 1588.

Denzinger, H.,—Bannwart, C.,—Umberg, J., *Enchiridion Symbolorum Definitionum et Declarationum de Rebus Fidei et Morum,* (DBU), ed., 18-20, Friburg: Herder, 1932.

Minge, J. *Patrologiae Cursus Completus, Series Latina,* (PL), 221 vols., Paris, 1844-1864.

Patrologiae Cursus Completus, Series Graeca, (PG) 161 vols., Paris, 1857-1866.

New Testament, ed., Confraternity of Christian Doctrine, Paterson: St. Anthony Guild, 1941.

Novum Testamentum, Graece et Latine, ed., 3 A. Merk, Rome: Pontifical Biblica Pontificel Institute, 1938.

Reference Works

Aertyns, J., *Theologia Moralis,* ed., 3, 2 vols., Tournay: Casterman. 1893.

Albert the Great, *Opera Omnia,* ed., A. Borgnet, 38 vols., Paris: Vives, 1890-1899.

Alexander of Hales, *Summa Theologica,* ed., B. Marrani, 3 vols., Ad Claras Aquas (Quaracchi): College of S. Bonaventure, 1930.

Antoine, P., *Theologia Moralis Universa,* 7 vols., in 3, Venice: Zotta, 1776.

Aquinas, T., St., *Basic Writings,* ed., A. Pegis, 2 vols., New York: Random, 1945.

Opera Omnia, ed., par. E. Frette et P. Mare, 34 vols., Paris: Vives, 1872-1880.

Opera Omnia, ed., Leo XIII, Rome: Sacra Cong. Prop. Fide, 1882-1930.

Aristotle, *The Basic Works of Aristotle,* ed., R. McKeon, New York: Random, 1941.

Astesano d'Aste, *Summa Astensis*, 2 vols., Rome: Menardi, 1728.

Azpilcueta, M., (Navarrus) *Opera Omnia*, 6 vols., Venice: Guerilium, 1618-1621.

Babenstuber, L., *Ethica Supernaturalis Salisburgensis sive Cursus Theologiae Moralis*, 2 vols., Augsbourg: Schluter & Happack, 1818.

Ballerini, A.,—Palmieri, D., *Opus Theologicum Morale*, ed., 2, 7 vols., Prati: Giachetti, 1892-1894.

Bannez, D., *De Fide, Spe, et Charitate*, Lyons: Michael, 1588.

Bertke, S., *The Possibility of Invincible Ignorance of the Natural Law*, Washington: Catholic University of America Press, 1941.

Billot, T., *De Virtutibus Infusis*, Rome: Gregorian, 1921.

Billuart, C., *Summa Sancti Thomae Hodiernis Academiarum Moribus Accomodata*, 8 vols., in 4, Paris: Palme, 1876.

Bonacina, M., *Opera De Morali Theologia*, 2 vols., Lyons: Prost, 1634.

Bonaventure, St., *Opera Omnia*, 10 vols., Ad Claras Aquas (Quaracchi): College of St. Bonaventure, 1882-1902.
Opera Omnia, ed., A. Peltier, 14 vols., Paris: Vives, 1864-1871.

Cajetan, T., *Commentaria in Summam Theologicam S. Thomae Aquinatis*, in the Leonine edition of St. Thomas' *Opera Omnia*, Rome: Sacra Cong. Prop. Fide, 1882-1930.
Summula Cajetani, Lyons: Gaspar, 1559.

Cappello, F., *Tractatus Canonico-Moralis De Sacramentis*, 3 vols., Turin: Marietti, 1938.

Capreolus, J., *Defensiones Theologiae*, 7 vols., Tours: Cattier, 1904.

Catalanus, P., *Universi Juris Theologico-Moralis Corpus Integrum*, 2 vols., Venice: Zane, 1728.

Cicero, M., *Laelius*, ed., E. Shuckburg—H. Johnston, New York: Macmillan, 1908.

Cicognani, A., *The Great Commandment in the Early Church*, tr., J. Scharde, Rome: Madre Di Dio, 1931.

Coccaleo, B., *Instituta Moralia*, 2 vols., Milan: Rizzardi, 1772.

Concina, D., *Theologia Christiana*, 2 vols., Bologne: Occhi 1756.

Daelman, C., *Theologia, seu Observationes Theologicae in Summam D. Thomae*, ed., 3, 9 vols., in 7, Lyons: Van Overbeke, 1759-1761.

D'Annibale, J., *Summula Theologiae Moralis*, ed., 3, 2 vols., Rome: Sacra Cong. Prop. Fide, 1891.

De Castropalao, F., *Opus Morale de Virtutibus et Vitiis Contrariis*, 2 vols., in 1, ed., novissima, Lyons: Barbier, 1682.

De Coninck, A., *De Moralitate, Natura et Effectibus Actuum Super-*

naturalium in Genere et Fide, Spe, ac Charitate Speciatim, Antwerp: Nutii, 1623.

De Ledesma, P., *Theologia Moralis,* Tournay: Quinque, 1636.

De Lugo J., *Disputationes Scholasticae et Morales,* ed., nova Fournials, 8 vols., Paris: Vives, 1868-1869.

De Medicis, J., *Formalis Explicatio Theologiae S. Thomae Aquinatis,* 10 vols., Vici: Soler, 1858-1862.

De Valentia, G., *Commentaria Theologica,* 4 vols., Ingolstad: Sortorius, 1603.

Denis the Carthusian, *Opera Omnia,* 41 vols., Tournay: Typis Carthusiae S. M. de Pratis, 1896-1912.

Fillion, J., *The New Psalter of the Roman Breviary,* St. Louis: Herder, 1915.

Gabriel a S. Vincentio, *De Remediis Ignorantiae,* Rome: Mancini, 1671.

Gatterer, H., *Compendium Theologiae Moralis,* Manz: Merani, 1889.

Genicot, E., *Theologiae Moralis Institutiones,* ed., 3, 2 vols., Louvain: Polleun-Ceuterick, 1900.

Gerson, J., *Opera Omnia,* 5 vols., Antwerp: Societatis, 1706.

Gobat, G., *Experientiae Theologico-Sacramentalis Explicatae,* Munich: Jaecklini, 1683.

Gonet, J., *Clypeus Theologiae Thomisticae,* 6 vols., Paris: Vives, 1876.

Gredt, J., *Elementa Philosophiae Aristotelico-Thomisticae,* ed., 7, 2 vols., Friburg: Herder, 1937.

Gutierrez, A., *Tractatus Scholasticus De Fide, Spe et Charitate,* Madrid: Rodrigues, 1728.

Heim, B., *Die Freundschaft nach Thomas von Aquin,* Rome: Angelicum, 1934.

Iorio, T., *Theologia Moralis,* ed., 3, 3 vols., Naples: D'Auria, 1946.

John of St. Thomas, *Cursus Philosophicus Thomisticus* ed., nova, 3 vols., Paris: Vives, 1883.

Lapide, C., a, *Commentaria In Scripturam Sacram,* ed., recens, 10 vols., Malta: Tonna-Branchi, 1851.

Lehmkuhl, A., *Theologia Moralis,* ed. 5, 2 vols., Friburg: Herder, 1888.

Liguori, A., St., *Homo Apostolicus,* Turin: Marietti, 1876.
   Theologia Moralis, ed., Le Noir, 4 vols., Paris: Vives, 1872.

Lombard, P., *Libri Quatuor Sententiarum* Paris: Vives, 1892.

Maldonatus, J., *Commentarii In Quatuor Evangelistas,* ed., Raich, 4 vols., Mainz: Kirchheim, 1874.

Mansi, J., *Epitome Doctrinae Moralis et Canonicae*, Malines: Hanicq, 1824.

Mausbach, J., *Catholic Moral Teaching and Its Antagonists*, tr., A. Buchanan, New York: Wagner, 1914.

Medina, B., *Expositio in Primam Secundam Angelici Doctoris*, Venice: Basam, 15-90.

Menoch, J., *Commentarius Totius Sacrae Scripturae*, 3 vols., 2, Venice: Remondi, 1771.

Merkelbach, B., *Summa Theologiae Moralis*, ed., 3, 3 vols., Paris: Desclée De Brouwer, 1938.

Michel, A., *Theologia Canonico-Moralis*, 2 vols., in 1, Augsbourg: Bencardi, 1707.

Moore, P., *Works of Peter of Poitiers*, Mediaeval Studies (1), Notre Dame: Notre Dame University Press, 1936.

Müller, E., *Theologia Moralis*, ed., 6, 3 vols., Vienna: Mayer, 1889-1891.

Natalis, A., *Theologia Dogmatica et Moralis secundum Ordinem Catechismi Tridentini*, 2 vols., Venice: Pezzana, 1705.

Noldin, H., *Summa Theologiae Moralis*, ed., 16, 3 vols., Innsbruck: Pustet, 1923.

Pereyra, B., *Promptuarium Theologicum Morale*, 2 vols., Evora: Academiae, 1703.

Pesch, C., *Praelectiones Dogmaticae*, 9 vols., Friburg: Herder, 1894-1899.

Peter of Poitiers, *Sententiae Petri Pictaviensis*, ed., P. Moore—M. Dulong, Mediaeval Studies (7) Notre Dame: Notre Dame University Press, 1943.

Pohle, J.,—Preuss, A., *God the Author of Nature and the Supernatural*, ed. 2, St. Louis: Herder, 1932.

Pontas, J., *Dictionarium Casuum Conscientiae*, ed., recens, 3 vols., Luxemburg: Chevalier & Bousquet, 1731-1732.

Porpora, A., *Theologia Moralis*, 4 vols., in 1, Naples: Manfredi, 1865.

Prümmer, D., *Manuale Theologiae Moralis*, ed., 10, 3 vols., Barcelona: Herder, 1946.

Reiffenstuel, A., *Jus Canonicum*, 7 vols., Paris: Vives, 1746.

Remer, V., *Summa Praelectionum Philosophiae Scholasticae*, 2 vols., Prati: Giachetti, 1900.

Rocafull, J., *Opus Morale In Decalogi Praeceptis et Ecclesiae Mandata*, Valentia: Sonzoni, 1649.

Ruland, L., *Morality and the Social Order*, tr. T. Rattler, St. Louis: Herder, 1942.

Salmanticensis Collegii, *Cursus Theologicus*, ed., nova correcta, 20 vols., Paris: Palma, 1870-1883.
Cursus Theologiae Moralis, 6 vols., in 3, Venice: Pezzana, 1728.

Sarra, H., *Memoriale Theologiae Moralis*, Rome: Merle, 1866.

Scotus, J., *Opera Omnia*, ed., nova, 26 vols., Paris: Vives, 1891-1895. 1891-1895.

Signoriello, N., *Lexicon Peripateticum Philosophico-Theologicum*, ed., 5, Rome: Pustet, 1931.

Sporer, P., *Theologia Moralis*, 3 vols., in 1, Salsbourg: Mayr, 1711.

Suarez, F., *Opera Omnia*, ed., nova (Andre-Berton), 26 vols., Paris: Vives, 1856-1861.

Sylvester, de Prierio (Mazolinus Sabaudus), *Summa Summarum*, 2 vols., Venice: Polum, 1601.

Sylvius, F., *Opera Omnia*, ed. novissima, 4 vols., Venice: Balleoniana, 1726.

Tanner, A., *Theologia Scholastica*, 4 vols., Ingolstad: Bayr, 1627.

Tanquerey, A., *Synopsis Theologiae Moralis et Pastoralis*, 3 vols., Paris: Desclee, 1936.

Thomas of Charmes, *Theologia Universa ad usum Sacrae Theologiae Candidatorum*, ed., 2, 7 vols., Florence: Formigli & Brazzini, 1761.

Tirinus, J., *Commentarius in Sacram Scripturam*, 2 vols., Lyons: De Ville, 1690.

Toletus, F., *In Summam Theologiae S. Thomae Aquinatis Enarratio*, 4 vols., Rome: Sacra Cong. Prop. Fide, 1869-1870.

Tudeschi, N., (Abbas Panormitanus), *Omnia quae extant Commentaria*, 8 vols., in 7, Venice: Juntas, 1578.

Valuy, B., *Fraternal Charity*, New York: Benzinger, 1908.

Van Steenkiste, J., *Sanctum Jesu Christi Evangelium Secundum Matthaeum*, ed., 3, 4 vols., in 2, Bruges: Desclée De Brouwer, 1880-1881.

Varceno, G.,—De Loiano, S., *Institutiones Theologiae Moralis*, 5 vols., Turin: Marietti, 1935.

Vasquez, G., *Commentariorum ac Disputationum in Primam Secundae Sancti Thomae*, ed., novissima, 2 vols., Lyons: Cardon, 1631.

Vermeersch, A., *Theologia Moralis*, 4 vols., Rome: Gregorian 1945.

Verricelli, A., *Quaestiones Morales et Legales*, Venice: Baba, 1653.

Wiggers, J., *Commentaria De Virtutibus Theologicis Fide, Spe, Charitate*, Louvain: Coenestini, 1666.

Willmers, C., *Institutiones Philosophiae*, 2 vols., Treves: S. Pauli, 1906.

Articles

Connell, F., "Adolescent Company Keeping," *The American Ecclesiastical Review*, 105, 6 (Dec. 1946) 458-459.

Delplace, L., "Wycliffe and his teaching concerning the Primacy," *Dublin Review*, 11 (3rd Series, 1884) 23-62.

Mandonet, P., "Chronologie sommaire de la vie et des escrits de s thomas," *Revue des sciences philosophiques et theologiques*, 9 (1920) 142-152.

INDEX

SUBJECT INDEX